RENT

RENT

The Complete Book and Lyrics
of the Broadway Musical

Book, Music, and Lyrics
by Jonathan Larson

Applause Theatre and Cinema Books
An Imprint of Hal Leonard Corporation
New York

Published in 2008 by Applause Theatre and Cinema Books
An Imprint of Hal Leonard Corporation
19 West 21st Street, New York, NY 10010

Book design by Lesley Kunikis

Library of Congress Cataloging-in-Publication Data
is available upon request.

ISBN 978-1-55783-737-0

www.applausepub.com

Contents

Introduction: *Rent* Is Real
by Victoria Leacock Hoffman...vii

Cast and Credits
(Original Broadway Performance)......................................xv

Musical Numbers...xix

Act One...1

Act Two...87

Introduction

Rent Is Real
by Victoria Leacock Hoffman

"*Rent* is about a community celebrating life in the face of death and
AIDS at the turn of the century."
—Jonathan Larson

When Jonathan Larson started writing *Rent*, he was twenty-nine
years old. It was 1989 and he was living in a fourth-floor tenement
walk-up on the edge of SoHo in downtown Manhattan.
People were dying.
AIDS seemed to be everywhere, and in New York City it was.
Jonathan's living room overlooked a garbage depot. Sitting at his
desk, a distressed drafting table, in his sagging director's chair, he
would devote almost seven years to creating his rock-musical *Rent*.
I had first met Jonathan Larson at Adelphi University in 1981,
during a rehearsal for the senior-class production of *Godspell*. He
was portraying Jesus and was being crucified. Since the musical was
being done with a "circus motif," he was being suspended above
the stage by two gymnastic rings. It is hard to sing and act when you
are hanging from your arms, and although I would soon discover
Jonathan's brilliance, at that moment he was struggling. I was a
freshman theatre major and had been assigned to focus lights for the
production. But I was focusing on Jonathan. I had heard about the
star of the senior show, how he had received a full four-year acting
scholarship and that he was also a great composer. And I liked what
I saw, his dark tussled hair and long limbs, and his impassioned
performance, despite the obvious physical discomfort, was arresting.
Just a few months earlier, there had been assassination attempts
against Pope John Paul II and President Reagan, and the first
anniversary of John Lennon's murder was approaching; the world
seemed an uncertain place. As I watched Jonathan sing his heart
out, I knew the world was a better place with him in it. I also knew
that he'd be my first love, which he was. What I didn't know was that
we would become best friends and close collaborators for the next
fifteen years.
In 1982, when Jonathan graduated and moved to Manhattan,
he intended to be an actor. He had started to go to open casting

calls for plays and musicals, but found his leading-man talent was being thwarted by his tall "character actor" looks. He had started a correspondence with Stephen Sondheim when he was in college, and after his first frustrating year in New York, he wrote to his mentor and asked if he thought he should pursue being a composer. Having critiqued some of Jonathan's music, the answer would change his life, for Sondheim told him, "I know a lot fewer starving composers then I do actors." Jonathan took the advice to mean that he was talented enough as a composer to try.

That same year, the Centers for Disease Control and Prevention gave a name to a new illness—AIDS (Acquired Immunodeficiency Syndrome). In New York, in the artistic community, there were whispers of a growing number of young gay men becoming ill and dying of rare cancers. Jonathan and I and our friends, some of whom were gay, started paying attention, but it was like seeing something out of the corner of your eye—we were aware of it, but until it was better defined and we knew what to do about it, we were absorbed in trying to pay our rent and forge our careers. AIDS, like auto accidents and plane crashes, was something you heard about, but only in terms of someone else: someone you didn't know.

Jonathan threw himself into writing musicals that he hoped and believed would save Broadway from itself. He had grown up in Westchester, just north of New York City, where his parents brought him and his sister, Julie, to see West Side Story, Gypsy, Hair, and Jesus Christ Superstar. But he was dismayed at what he now saw as the pandering of Broadway to busloads of lunching blue-haired ladies. The shows he had been raised on had been replaced by pyrotechnic spectacles and whiskery costumes. He believed theatre should be transcendent, with the power to change your life. And he believed he was the man to do it.

To this end, he waited tables at Hamburger Harry's, in the theatre district, where he met and began dating Brenda Daniels, fellow waitperson and modern dancer. She was tall, with short, spiky hair, and had tremendous talent. She was teaching at the Merce Cunningham Studio and was well aware of the threat that was enveloping her community of dancers: HIV, the human immunodeficiency virus, had been identified as the virus that causes AIDS. And it was tearing through the lives of the dance company, like it would in the fashion, nightclub, theatre, and film communities. Rock Hudson, a very handsome matinee idol of Jon's mother's generation, had shocked much of the nation when shortly before he died he disclosed he had AIDS. His ravaged appearance underscored the viciousness of the illness.

Throughout the mid-eighties, as the hole in the ozone layer grew, celebrities were trying to heal the world's ills with the pop songs "Do They Know It's Christmas" and "We Are the World." In New York City, crack cocaine had started to work its way into the lives of the vulnerable, and the homeless population was exploding, with almost 25,000 people living on the streets and in the shelter system. Jonathan, who subscribed to the *New York Times* no matter how poor he was, absorbed these facts and saw many of them outside his window while living with two roommates, two cats and working his three shifts a week, now at the Moondance Diner. He spent the rest of his time, writing a musical version of George Orwell's *1984* that he'd been unable to secure the rights for, and *Superbia*, a futuristic allegory about bottom-line mentality in an orbiting studio where everyone lives on and for the camera. Both musicals were set in a world where Big Brother greed and lust for power supersedes the individual's hopes and dreams.

The heroes Jonathan created kept trying to restore those hopes and dreams. And in pursuit of his own, he had developed good relationships with ASCAP and the Dramatists Guild, being invited to workshop his material.

But in 1986, nothing he could have imagined would have prepared him for the news that his childhood best friend, Matt O'Grady, was about to tell him when he arrived at the Moondance Diner and ordered a milk shake. Best friends since they were six, they had played on their tree-lined street and swum in the neighbors' pools. Matt's welcoming Irish Catholic family blended seamlessly with the liberal Jewish Larsons, and theirs were, perhaps, the only two families in White Plains to vote for George McGovern in 1972. They went to school together, and in high school, when Matt realized he was gay, the first person he told was Jonathan. Jon never judged, he listened and cared. So that day, when Matt settled in at the counter at the Moondance, as he often did for a visit with Jon, all seemed well. But Matt had news; he was HIV positive. For Jon, in that moment, HIV had gone from being in articles in the *New York Times* and the wrenching stories of friends' friends wasting away and dying from AIDS to looking into his best friend's eyes and praying that Matt would somehow survive. It was an apocalyptic disease. For the

28,712 people in the United States who had progressed from being HIV positive to having AIDS by 1986, 24,559 had died by year's end. Matt's diagnosis had a profound impact on Jonathan's life. It would accelerate everything, because, I believe, it started an invisible stopwatch. Time could run out.

By 1989, a year after Libyan terrorists had brought down Pan Am Flight 103 over Lockerbie, Scotland, and medical waste had started washing up on the beaches of Long Island, people were listening to Bobby McFerrin's "Don't Worry, Be Happy" and trying the antidepressant Prozac. Jonathan had won several prestigious awards and grants for Superbia, but with each new draft, his hero's and heroine's outcomes diminished. In a late draft, his heroine chooses to electrocute herself by touching the wires inside her MT (media transmitter) and the hero decides not to save the world. Jon was frustrated with the progress of his career. He was about to turn thirty, was in a committed relationship with another beautiful dancer, Janet Charleston, and was still waiting tables at the Moondance Diner. And though, to Jonathan's relief, Matt O'Grady was doing well and his HIV had not progressed to AIDS, the number of reported AIDS cases had quadrupled to 117,508. One of those new cases was our good friend Alison Gertz. Ali's diagnosis and the discovery that she had become infected when she was sixteen from a single sexual encounter with a boyfriend became international news. At twenty-two she became the new face of AIDS. It was the year the Exxon Valdez spilled 11 million gallons of crude oil onto the shores of Alaska and hundreds, if not thousands, of young people were killed during student protests in China's Tiananmen Square. Jon needed to say something, and though he had written many political cabarets for Adelphi University, he was anxious to start work on a new show that would create a platform for the many social issues that troubled him.

That summer, Ira Weitzman, the musical theatre program director of Playwrights Horizons (the nonprofit theatre where Sondheim would develop many of his shows and Jonathan had received a workshop of Superbia), recommended Jonathan to playwright Billy Aronson, who was interested in creating a modern musical based on Puccini's La Bohème. After listening to some of Jonathan's music, they agreed to meet.

Billy arrived at Jon's place on Greenwich Street shortly before dusk. Since there was no doorbell, he called from the pay phone on the corner and Jon threw down the keys. Billy made his way through the smudged halls, up the three flights of rickety stairs to meet Jon in his kitchen, which had a large four-legged bathtub in the center of it. They got some lemonade and seltzer and climbed a steep ladder to the roof. Overlooking the Hudson River, as the lights of the prison barge appeared (New York had run out of space for its more violent offenders), Billy, sitting on a crate, shared his own frustrations and fears about the arts and theatre and life.

They agreed to work together and eventually wrote first drafts of the songs "Rent," "Santa Fe," and "I Should Tell You." They were both excited by the feel of the pieces and the vibrancy of the music. Jon suggested the title *Rent* and reminded Billy of its other definition: to tear apart with force or violence, an apt metaphor for the turmoil in the community they were describing. From that first meeting, Jon had strong ideas about many aspects of the show that exist in its final form, from the East Village location to the drug addiction of Mimi, and most importantly, that she lives. He felt very strongly that the show was about celebrating life. And as he and Billy continued to work into November, when the Berlin Wall fell and trumpeted the beginning of the end of the Cold War, it seemed that there may well be things to celebrate. The reinventing of a great classic like Puccini's *La Bohème*, based on Henri Murger's book *Scenes de la Vie Bohème*, with tuberculoses in Paris in the 1800s being replaced with AIDS in New York City at the end of the twentieth century, was the canvas Jon's creativity had been longing for. But as Billy and he continued to try to work through the story, with both of them new to collaborating, they found their essentially different writing styles were at odds. After a few months of working together, they recorded a demo of the first three songs and decided to pursue different projects individually.

There was another reason that Jon took a step away from *Rent*. He was anxious about creating another large-scale musical that producers would shy away from. For five years, including that past September with a well-attended concert version at the Village Gate, he had heard that *Superbia*, with its large cast and futuristic sets, would be dauntingly expensive to produce. Jonathan wanted to pare down his next show. The New Year arrived, and his thirtieth birthday was celebrated with a surprise party I threw at our friend Pam Shaw's landlady's West Village brownstone (what we couldn't provide ourselves, we borrowed!). Though Matt and many of his closest friends attended, our friend Gordon couldn't. He had been admitted to the hospital that week. At 6 feet 7 inches, the usually robust and stylish Gordon, who had worked on the costumes for the recent *Superbia* concert, was on a respirator, being fed through a tube in his nose, and was paralyzed from the neck down. He had a rare ailment unusual in a healthy twenty-eight-year-old, so the doctors asked him to take an HIV test. By the time they informed him that he had full-blown AIDS two weeks later, he was a skeletal 127 pounds. He was unable to speak for the first three months of his diagnosis. He was one of the 160,969 cases of AIDS reported in the United States by the end of 1990.

Jonathan, who was very emotionally connected to his friends and surroundings, set to work on a new form of musical, a "rock monologue" that he would perform himself with a four-piece band. He had been inspired by the personal and political monologues of Eric Bogosian and Spalding Gray and the performance pieces of Laurie Anderson. He would write a multi-titled piece he would eventually call *tick, tick . . . BOOM!* that would tell the very semi-autobiographical story of a composer named *Jonathan* during the week of his thirtieth birthday, exploring his fear that he would never fulfill his dream of "being the future of the American musical" and examining how his life changes when he learns that his best friend is HIV positive. Ultimately, the character *Jonathan* is empowered to try to change the world through his writing.

Jon and I staged a small production of *tick, tick . . . BOOM!* at the Second Stage Theatre and several workshops for a young producer named Jeffrey Seller, but we were finding it as difficult to get a theatrical production for this much leaner show as we'd had with *Superbia*. In a last-ditch attempt, we hoped to launch a successful ongoing run at the Village Gate in November 1991. We had raised some money (much of it our own) and were paying a band to perform with Jonathan. On a cold Wednesday night, I arrived at the Night Owl Studios on West 30th Street during the first, and only, full-band rehearsal with Jonathan and our director, Pippin Parker. I avoided eye contact with Jonathan and called Pippin out of the room. I was weak and distressed and didn't know what to do; Pamela Shaw, whom I had known since I was six and Jon had dated, had just found out that she had AIDS. We could hear Jon singing through the studio door. He sounded amazing as he sang a wrenching version of "Why," about his friendship with Matt. Pippin and I agreed that

I should not tell him until after opening night. This was not only shocking news but meant that Jonathan had been exposed to the virus and needed to be tested himself.

The opening was well attended and Jon was glad to be performing again. After a celebratory late-night dinner, I walked him back to the edge of SoHo and joined him for what he thought would be a nightcap to discuss the evening's events. I told Jon to sit down.

I told him that Pam had been tested for HIV because of a minor infection in her mouth. I told him that she was HIV positive, and though she appeared perfectly healthy, she had six of the 1,000-plus T cells per microliter that a healthy person has and essentially had no immune system, and therefore she had AIDS. I told him that he needed to be tested. Jonathan was speechless. He was truly shaken by Pam's diagnosis and as frightened as anyone would be to find out that they have been exposed to the deadly virus. In a few weeks, he was relieved to find out he was HIV negative, but it was no time to celebrate. The grim reality that four of our best friends were infected with HIV, and three of them had developed AIDS, changed everything in our lives. Jon hosted a peasants feast every year—a giant potluck holiday meal for his artist friends and extended family—and that year each toast filled our eyes with tears.

That fall, Jonathan asked Billy Aronson for permission to proceed with *Rent* on his own. Permission was granted. And from that time on, Jon threw himself into *Rent*, a canvas large enough to honor his friends and to raise awareness about AIDS and the social injustices he saw every day. As he would proclaim in his song "La Vie Boheme," "the opposite of war isn't peace, it's creation."

That is what Jonathan did, he created *Rent*, and everything he felt and feared and celebrated is in this libretto. And it is filled with his love, too. In the early hours of January 25, 1996, after the final dress rehearsal for *Rent* at the New York Theatre Workshop in the East Village, elated and exhausted, Jonathan made his way home. He died, alone in his apartment, from a dissecting aortic aneurysm that doctors in two hospital emergency rooms had failed to detect. He never knew that *Rent* would indeed change the American musical theatre. But I know he would be proud that it did.

Cast and Credits

RENT

Book, Music, and Lyrics by Jonathan Larson
Directed by Michael Greif

Rent was originally produced in New York by New York Theatre Workshop and on Broadway by Jeffrey Seller, Kevin McCollum, Allan S. Gordon, and New York Theatre Workshop.

Original Broadway Performance

Cast in order of appearance:

ROGER DAVIS
Adam Pascal

MARK COHEN
Anthony Rapp

TOM COLLINS
Jesse L. Martin

BENJAMIN COFFIN III
Taye Diggs

JOANNE JEFFERSON
Fredi Walker

ANGEL DUMOTT SCHUNARD
Wilson Jermaine Heredia

MIMI MARQUEZ
Daphne Rubin-Vega

MAUREEN JOHNSON
Idina Menzel

MARK'S MOM AND OTHERS
Kristen Lee Kelly

MR. JEFFERSON, SOLOIST #2, CAROLER, A PASTOR, AND OTHERS
Byron Utley

MRS. JEFFERSON, SOLOIST #1, WOMAN WITH BAGS, AND OTHERS
Gwen Stewart

GORDON, THE MAN, MR. GREY, AND OTHERS
Timothy Britten Parker

STEVE, MAN WITH SQUEEGEE, A WAITER, AND OTHERS
Gilles Chiasson

PAUL, POLICE OFFICER, AND OTHERS
Rodney Hicks

ALEXI DARLING, ROGER'S MOM, AND OTHERS
Aiko Nakasone

Understudies
Yassmin Alers, Darius de Haas, Shelly Dickinson, Norbert Leo Butz,
Mark Setlock, and Shayna Steele

Set Design
Paul Clay

Costume Design
Angela Wendt

Lighting Design
Blake Burba

Sound Design
Kurt Fischer

Original Concept and Additional Lyrics
Billy Aronson

Musical Arrangements
Steve Skinner

Publicity
Richard Kornberg and Don Summa

Casting
Bernard Telsey Casting

Technical Supervision
Unitech Productions, Inc.

General Management
Emanuel Azenberg and John Corker

Production Stage Manager
John Vivian

Music Supervision and Additional Arrangements
Tim Weil

Choreography
Marlies Yearby

Dramaturg
Lynn M. Thomson

The Band:

Conductor, Piano, and Synthesizers
Tim Weil

Bass
Steve Mack

Guitars
Kenny Brescia

Drums and Percussion
Jeff Potter

Keyboards and Guitars
Daniel A. Weiss

Musical Numbers

Act One

1. Tune Up #1	Mark
2. Voice Mail #1	Mrs. Cohen
3. Tune Up #2	Mark, Roger, Collins, and Benny
4. Rent	The Company
5. You Okay, Honey?	Angel and Collins
6. Tune Up #3	Mark and Roger
7. One Song Glory	Roger
8. Light My Candle	Roger and Mimi
9. Voice Mail #2	Mr. and Mrs. Jefferson
10. Today 4 U	Mark, Collins, Roger, and Angel
11. You'll See	Benny, Mark, Collins, Roger, and Angel
12. Tango: Maureen	Mark and Joanne
13. Life Support	Paul, Gordon, and the Company
14. Out Tonight	Mimi
15. Another Day	Roger, Mimi, and the Company
16. Will I?	Steve and the Company
17. X-Mo Bells #2/Bummer	The Company
18. Santa Fe	Collins and the Company
19. I'll Cover You	Angel and Collins
20. We're Okay	Joanne
21. Christmas Bells	The Company
22. Over the Moon	Maureen
23. La Vie Bohème	The Company
24. I Should Tell You	Roger and Mimi
25. La Vie Bohème B	The Company

Act Two

26. Seasons of Love   The Company
27. Happy New Year   Mark, Mimi, Roger, Maureen,
                             Joanne, Collins, and Angel
28. Voice Mail #3   Mrs. Cohen and Alexi Darling
29. Happy New Year B   Maureen, Mark, Joanne, Benny,
                             Roger, Mimi, Angel, Collins,
                             and the Man
30. Take Me or Leave Me   Maureen and Joanne
31. Seasons of Love B   The Company
32. Without You   Roger and Mimi
33. Voice Mail #4   Alexi Darling
34. Contact   The Company
35. I'll Cover You: Reprise Collins and the Company
36. Halloween   Mark
37. Goodbye, Love   Mark, Mimi, Roger, Maureen,
                             Joanne, Collins, and Benny
38. What You Own   Pastor, Mark, Collins, Benny,
                             and Roger
39. Voice Mail #5   Roger's Mom, Mimi's Mom,
                             Mr. Jefferson, and Mrs. Cohen
40. Finale A   The Company
41. Your Eyes   Roger
42. Finale B   The Company

Spoken lines are set in upper- and lowercase. The libretto is published as performed on Broadway at the Nederlander Theatre, April 29, 1996. Variations may occur during a performance.

RENT

Act One

(The audience enters the theatre to discover the curtainless set. The one set piece onstage, at stage left, is a huge tower that represents (a) a totem pole/Christmas tree that stands in an abandoned lot, (b) a wood stove with a snaky chimney that is at the center of MARK and ROGER's loft apartment, and (c) the steeple of a church in ACT TWO. There is a wooden platform loft area at stage right with a railing around it, under which sits the band of five musicians. It has a staircase on the upstage side. Downstage is a black, waist-high rail fence.)

(Onstage, once the house is open, CREW and BAND MEMBERS move about informally in preparation for the play.)

(ROGER enters from upstage left with an electric guitar and crosses to a guitar amp sitting on a chair at center stage. He casually plugs his guitar into the amp and sets levels, then crosses downstage and sits on the table.)

(After a few beats, the COMPANY, led by MARK, enters from all directions and fills the stage. MARK sets up a small tripod and a 16mm movie camera downstage center, aimed upstage. He addresses the audience.)

MARK
We begin on Christmas Eve, with me, Mark, and my roommate, Roger. We live in an industrial loft on the corner of 11th Street and Avenue B, the top floor of what was once a music publishing factory. Old rock 'n' roll posters hang on the walls. They have Roger's picture advertising gigs at CBGB's and the Pyramid Club. We have an illegal wood-burning stove; its exhaust pipe crawls up to a skylight. All of our electrical appliances are plugged into one thick extension cord, which snakes its way out a window. Outside, a small tent city has sprung up in the lot next to our building. Inside, we are freezing because we have no heat.

(HE turns the camera to ROGER.)

Smile!

1. Tune Up #1

MARK

DECEMBER 24. NINE PM.
EASTERN STANDARD TIME
FROM HERE ON IN
I SHOOT WITHOUT A SCRIPT
SEE IF ANYTHING COMES OF IT
INSTEAD OF MY OLD SHIT

FIRST SHOT—ROGER
TUNING THE FENDER GUITAR
HE HASN'T PLAYED IN A YEAR

ROGER

THIS WON'T TUNE

MARK

SO WE HEAR
HE'S JUST COMING BACK
FROM HALF A YEAR OF WITHDRAWAL

ROGER

ARE YOU TALKING TO ME?

MARK

NOT AT ALL
ARE YOU READY? HOLD THAT FOCUS—STEADY
TELL THE FOLKS AT HOME WHAT YOU'RE DOING, ROGER . . .

ROGER

I'M WRITING ONE GREAT—

MARK

The phone rings.

ROGER

SAVED!

MARK
(to audience)

WE SCREEN
ZOOM IN ON THE ANSWERING MACHINE!

(An actor sets a telephone on a chair and we see MARK'S MOM in a special light.)

2. Voice Mail #1

ROGER and MARK'S ANSWERING MACHINE

SPEAK
(BEEEEP!)

MOM

THAT WAS A VERY LOUD BEEP
I DON'T EVEN KNOW IF THIS IS WORKING
MARK—MARK—ARE YOU THERE
ARE YOU SCREENING YOUR CALLS—IT'S MOM

WE WANTED TO CALL AND SAY WE LOVE YOU
AND WE'LL MISS YOU TOMORROW
CINDY AND THE KIDS ARE HERE—SEND THEIR LOVE
OH, I HOPE YOU LIKE THE HOT PLATE

JUST DON'T LEAVE IT ON, DEAR
WHEN YOU LEAVE THE HOUSE

OH, AND, MARK
WE'RE SORRY TO HEAR THAT MAUREEN DUMPED YOU
I SAY, C'EST LA VIE
SO LET HER BE A LESBIAN
THERE ARE OTHER FISHIES IN THE SEA

. . . LOVE, MOM

(Lights fade on MOM and answering machine.)

3. Tune Up #2

MARK
TELL THE FOLKS AT HOME WHAT YOU'RE DOING, ROGER . . .

ROGER
I'M WRITING ONE GREAT SONG—

MARK
(to audience)
The phone rings.

ROGER
Yesss!

MARK
(to audience)
We screen.

ROGER and MARK'S ANSWERING MACHINE
SPEAK
(BEEEEP!)

(Lights fade up on THE STREET, the front-door area of the boys building. A battered public phone is nearby. TOM COLLINS stands at the phone.)

COLLINS
"CHESTNUTS ROASTING—"

ROGER and MARK
(as MARK picks up the phone)
COLLINS!

COLLINS
I'M DOWNSTAIRS.

MARK
HEY!

COLLINS

ROGER PICKED UP THE PHONE?

MARK

NO, IT'S ME

COLLINS

THROW DOWN THE KEY

(MARK pulls out a small leather pouch and drops it off the apron downstage center as if out a window, just as a weighted leather pouch plops down from "upstairs." COLLINS catches it.)

MARK

A WILD NIGHT IS NOW PREORDAINED

(Two THUGS appear from above with clubs. They are obviously close to attacking COLLINS, who says back into the phone . . .)

COLLINS

I MAY BE DETAINED

(THUGS mime beating and kicking COLLINS, who falls to the ground as lights on him fade.)

MARK

WHAT DOES HE MEAN . . . ?
                    (Phone rings again)
WHAT DO YOU MEAN –"DETAINED??

(Lights come up on BENNY, who is on a cell phone.)

BENNY

HO HO HO

MARK and ROGER

BENNY! (SHIT!)

BENNY

DUDES, I'M ON MY WAY

MARK and ROGER
GREAT! (FUCK!)

BENNY
I NEED THE RENT

MARK
WHAT RENT?

BENNY
THIS PAST YEAR'S RENT, WHICH I LET SLIDE

MARK
LET SLIDE? YOU SAID WE WERE "GOLDEN"

ROGER
WHEN YOU BOUGHT THE BUILDING

MARK
WHEN WE WERE ROOMMATES

ROGER
REMEMBER—YOU LIVED HERE!?

BENNY
HOW COULD I FORGET?
YOU, ME, COLLINS AND MAUREEN
HOW IS THE DRAMA QUEEN?

MARK
SHE'S PERFORMING TONIGHT

BENNY
I KNOW
STILL HER PRODUCTION MANAGER?

MARK
TWO DAYS AGO I WAS BUMPED

BENNY

YOU STILL DATING HER?

MARK

LAST MONTH I WAS DUMPED

ROGER

SHE'S IN LOVE

BENNY

SHE'S GOT A NEW MAN?

MARK

WELL—NO

BENNY

WHAT'S HIS NAME?

MARK and ROGER

JOANNE

BENNY

RENT, MY AMIGOS, IS DUE
OR I WILL HAVE TO EVICT YOU
BE THERE IN A FEW

(ROGER defiantly picks out Musetta's theme from *La Bohème* on the electric guitar. The fuse blows on the amp.)

MARK

The power blows . . .

(The COMPANY bursts into a flurry of movement and all but MARK and ROGER freeze in a group upstage.)

4. Rent

MARK
HOW DO YOU DOCUMENT REAL LIFE
WHEN REAL LIFE'S GETTING MORE
LIKE FICTION EACH DAY
HEADLINES—BREADLINES
BLOW MY MIND
AND NOW THIS DEADLINE
"EVICTION—OR PAY"
RENT

ROGER
HOW DO YOU WRITE A SONG
WHEN THE CHORDS SOUND WRONG
THOUGH THEY ONCE SOUNDED RIGHT AND RARE
WHEN THE NOTES ARE SOUR
WHERE IS THE POWER
YOU ONCE HAD TO IGNITE THE AIR

MARK
AND WE'RE HUNGRY AND FROZEN

ROGER
SOME LIFE THAT WE'VE CHOSEN

MARK and ROGER
HOW WE GONNA PAY
HOW WE GONNA PAY
HOW WE GONNA PAY
LAST YEAR'S RENT

MARK
(to audience)
WE LIGHT CANDLES

ROGER
HOW DO YOU START A FIRE
WHEN THERE'S NOTHING TO BURN
AND IT FEELS LIKE SOMETHING'S STUCK IN YOUR FLUE

MARK
HOW CAN YOU GENERATE HEAT
WHEN YOU CAN'T FEEL YOUR FEET

MARK and ROGER
AND THEY'RE TURNING BLUE!

MARK
YOU LIGHT UP A MEAN BLAZE

(ROGER grabs one of his own posters.)

ROGER
WITH POSTERS—

(MARK grabs old manuscripts.)

MARK
AND SCREENPLAYS

MARK and ROGER
HOW WE GONNA PAY
HOW WE GONNA PAY
HOW WE GONNA PAY
LAST YEAR'S RENT

(Lights go down on loft and go up on JOANNE JEFFERSON, who's at the pay phone.)

JOANNE
DON'T SCREEN, MAUREEN
IT'S ME—JOANNE
YOUR SUBSTITUTE PRODUCTION MANAGER
HEY HEY HEY! (DID YOU EAT?)
DON'T CHANGE THE SUBJECT, MAUREEN
BUT, DARLING—YOU HAVEN'T EATEN ALL DAY

YOU WON'T THROW UP
YOU WON'T THROW UP
THE DIGITAL DELAY—

DIDN'T BLOW UP (EXACTLY)
THERE MAY HAVE BEEN ONE TEENY TINY SPARK
YOU'RE NOT CALLING MARK

(Lights go up on COLLINS, who struggles and stands.)

COLLINS
HOW DO YOU STAY ON YOUR FEET
WHEN ON EVERY STREET
IT'S "TRICK OR TREAT"
(AND TONIGHT IT'S "TRICK")
"WELCOME BACK TO TOWN"
I SHOULD LIE DOWN
EVERYTHING'S BROWN
AND UH—OH
I FEEL SICK

MARK
(at the window)
WHERE IS HE?

COLLINS
GETTING DIZZY
(He collapses.)

MARK and ROGER
HOW WE GONNA PAY
HOW WE GONNA PAY
HOW WE GONNA PAY
LAST YEAR'S RENT

(MARK and ROGER stoke the fire. Crosscut to BENNY's Range Rover.)

BENNY
(on cell phone)
ALISON, BABY—YOU SOUND SAD
I CAN'T BELIEVE THOSE TWO
AFTER EVERYTHING I'VE DONE

EVER SINCE OUR WEDDING
I'M DIRT—THEY'LL SEE
I CAN HELP THEM ALL OUT IN THE LONG RUN

(Three locales: JOANNE at the pay phone, MARK and ROGER
at the loft, and COLLINS on the ground. The following is sung
simultaneously.)

BENNY

FORCES ARE GATHERING
FORCES ARE GATHERING
CAN'T TURN AWAY
FORCES ARE GATHERING

COLLINS

UGHHHH
UGHHHH—
UGHHHH—I CAN'T THINK
UGHHHH—
UGHHHH—
UGHHHH—I NEED A DRINK

MARK
(reading from a script page)
"THE MUSIC IGNITES THE NIGHT WITH PASSIONATE FIRE"

JOANNE
MAUREE—I'M NOT A THEATRE PERSON

ROGER
"THE NARRATION CRACKLES AND POPS WITH INCENDIARY WIT"

JOANNE
COULD NEVER BE A THEATRE PERSON

MARK
(to audience)
ZOOM IN AS THEY BURN THE PAST TO THE GROUND

JOANNE
(realizing she's been cut off)
HELLO?

MARK and ROGER
AND FEEL THE HEAT OF THE FUTURE'S GLOW

JOANNE
HELLO?

(The phone rings in the loft. MARK picks it up.)

MARK
HELLO? MAUREEN?
YOUR EQUIPMENT WON'T WORK?
OKAY, ALL RIGHT, I'LL GO!

MARK and HALF THE COMPANY
HOW DO YOU LEAVE THE PAST BEHIND
WHEN IT KEEPS FINDING WAYS TO GET TO YOUR HEART
IT REACHES WAY DOWN DEEP AND TEARS YOU INSIDE OUT
'TIL YOU'RE TORN APART
RENT

ROGER and OTHER HALF OF COMPANY
HOW CAN YOU CONNECT IN AN AGE
WHERE STRANGERS, LANDLORDS, LOVERS
YOUR OWN BLOOD CELLS BETRAY

ALL
WHAT BINDS THE FABRIC TOGETHER
WHEN THE RAGING, SHIFTING WINDS OF CHANGE
KEEP RIPPING AWAY

BENNY
DRAW A LINE IN THE SAND
AND THEN MAKE A STAND

ROGER
USE YOUR CAMERA TO SPAR

MARK

USE YOUR GUITAR

ALL

WHEN THEY ACT TOUGH—YOU CALL THEIR BLUFF

MARK and ROGER

WE'RE NOT GONNA PAY

MARK, ROGER, and HALF THE COMPANY

WE'RE NOT GONNA PAY

MARK, ROGER, and OTHER HALF OF COMPANY

WE'RE NOT GONNA PAY

ALL

LAST YEAR'S RENT
THIS YEAR'S RENT
NEXT YEAR'S RENT
RENT, RENT, RENT, RENT, RENT
WE'RE NOT GONNA PAY RENT

ROGER and MARK

'CAUSE EVERYTHING IS RENT

5. You Okay, Honey?

The Street: in front of the pay phone

(A HOMELESS MAN appears above on the right. Across the stage, sitting on the Christmas tree sculpture is ANGEL DUMOTT SCHUNARD, with a plastic pickle tub balanced like a drum between his knees.)

HOMELESS MAN

CHRISTMAS BELLS ARE RINGING
CHRISTMAS BELLS ARE RINGING
CHRISTMAS BELLS ARE RINGING

SOMEWHERE ELSE
NOT HERE

(The HOMELESS MAN exits. ANGEL gets a good beat going on the
tub until a moan interrupts him. He starts to drum again and sees
COLLINS limp to downstage-left proscenium.)

ANGEL
YOU OKAY, HONEY?

COLLINS
I'M AFRAID SO

ANGEL
THEY GET ANY MONEY?

COLLINS
NO, HAD NONE TO GET
BUT THEY PURLOINED MY COAT
WELL YOU MISSED A SLEEVE! THANKS

ANGEL
HELL, IT'S CHRISTMAS EVE
I'M ANGEL

COLLINS
ANGEL? INDEED
AN ANGEL OF THE FIRST DEGREE
FRIENDS CALL ME COLLINS—TOM COLLINS
NICE TREE . . .

ANGEL
LET'S GET A BAND-AID FOR YOUR KNEE
I'LL CHANGE, THERE'S A "LIFE SUPPORT" MEETING
AT NINE THIRTY
YES, THIS BODY PROVIDES A COMFORTABLE HOME
FOR THE ACQUIRED IMMUNE DEFICIENCY SYNDROME

COLLINS
AS DOES MINE

                    ANGEL
WE'LL GET ALONG FINE
GET YOU A COAT, HAVE A BITE
MAKE A NIGHT—I'M FLUSH

                  COLLINS
MY FRIENDS ARE WAITING—

                    ANGEL
YOU'RE CUTE WHEN YOU BLUSH
THE MORE THE MERRY—HO HO HO
AND I DO NOT TAKE NO

(ANGEL and COLLINS walk off stage right, lights up on loft.)

6. Tune Up #3

                  ROGER
Where are you going?

                  MARK
Maureen calls.

                  ROGER
You're such a sucker.

                  MARK
I don't suppose you'd like to see her show in the lot tonight?
(ROGER shrugs)
Or come to dinner?

                  ROGER
Zoom in on my empty wallet.

                  MARK
Touché. Take your AZT.
                  (to audience)
CLOSE ON ROGER

HIS GIRLFRIEND APRIL
LEFT A NOTE SAYING, "WE'VE GOT AIDS"
BEFORE SLITTING HER WRISTS IN THE BATHROOM

I'll check up on you later. Change your mind. You have to get out of the house.

7. One Song Glory

ROGER

I'M WRITING ON GREAT SONG BEFORE I . . .
ONE SONG
GLORY
ONE SONG
BEFORE I GO
GLORY
ONE SONG TO LEAVE BEHIND

FIND ONE SONG
ONE LAST REFRAIN
GLORY
FROM THE PRETTY-BOY FRONT MAN
WHO WASTED OPPORTUNITY

ONE SONG
HE HAD THE WORLD AT HIS FEET
GLORY
IN THE EYES OF A YOUNG GIRL
A YOUNG GIRL
FIND GLORY
BEYOND THE CHEAP COLORED LIGHTS

ONE SONG
BEFORE THE SUN SETS
GLORY—ON ANOTHER EMPTY LIFE
TIME FLIES—TIME DIES
GLORY—ONE BLAZE OF GLORY
ONE BLAZE OF GLORY—GLORY

FIND
GLORY
IN A SONG THAT RINGS TRUE
TRUTH LIKE A BLAZING FIRE
AN ETERNAL FLAME

FIND
ONE SONG
A SONG ABOUT LOVE
GLORY
FROM THE SOUL OF A YOUNG MAN
A YOUNG MAN

FIND
THE ONE SONG
BEFORE THE VIRUS TAKES HOLD
GLORY
LIKE A SUNSET
ONE SONG
TO REDEEM THIS EMPTY LIFE

TIME FLIES
AND THEN—NO NEED TO ENDURE ANYMORE
TIME DIES

(ROGER is interrupted by a sharp knock on the door. It is MIMI
MARQUEZ, a beautiful stranger from downstairs.)

ROGER

The door.

(ROGER crosses to the door.)

8. Light My Candle

ROGER
WHAT'D YOU FORGET?

(MIMI enters, holding a candle and looking for a match.)

MIMI
GOT A LIGHT?

ROGER
I KNOW YOU—YOU'RE—
YOU'RE SHIVERING

MIMI
IT'S NOTHING
THEY TURNED OFF MY HEAT
AND I'M JUST A LITTLE
WEAK ON MY FEET
WOULD YOU LIGHT MY CANDLE?
WHAT ARE YOU STARING AT?

ROGER
NOTHING
YOUR HAIR IN THE MOONLIGHT
YOU LOOK FAMILIAR

(ROGER lights her candle. MIMI starts to leave, but stumbles.)

ROGER
CAN YOU MAKE IT?

MIMI
JUST HAVEN'T EATEN MUCH TODAY
AT LEAST THE ROOM STOPPED SPINNING. ANYWAY. WHAT?

ROGER
NOTHING
YOUR SMILE REMINDED ME OF—

MIMI

I ALWAYS REMIND PEOPLE OF—WHO IS SHE?

ROGER

SHE DIED. HER NAME WAS APRIL

(MIMI discretely blows out the candle.)

MIMI

IT'S OUT AGAIN
SORRY ABOUT YOUR FRIEND
WOULD YOU LIGHT MY CANDLE?

(ROGER lights the candle. They linger, awkwardly.)

ROGER

WELL—

MIMI

YEAH. OW!

ROGER

OH. THE WAX—IT'S—

MIMI

DRIPPING! I LIKE IT—BETWEEN MY—

ROGER

FINGERS. I FIGURED . . .
OH, WELL. GOOD NIGHT

(MIMI exits. ROGER starts toward his guitar. Another knock.
ROGER answers it.)

ROGER

IT BLEW OUT AGAIN?

MIMI

NO—I THINK THAT I DROPPED MY STASH

ROGER

I KNOW I'VE SEEN YOU OUT AND ABOUT
WHEN I USED TO GO OUT
YOUR CANDLE'S OUT

MIMI

I'M ILLIN'—I HAD IT WHEN I WALKED IN THE DOOR
IT WAS PURE—IS IT ON THE FLOOR?

ROGER

THE FLOOR?

(MIMI gets down on all fours and starts looking for her stash.
She looks back at ROGER, and he's staring at her again.)

MIMI

THEY SAY I HAVE THE BEST ASS BELOW 14TH STREET
IS IT TRUE?

ROGER

WHAT?

MIMI

YOU'RE STARING AGAIN

ROGER

OH NO.
I MEAN YOU DO—HAVE A NICE—
I MEAN—YOU LOOK FAMILIAR

MIMI

LIKE YOU'RE DEAD GIRLFRIEND?

ROGER

ONLY WHEN YOU SMILE
BUT I'M SURE I'VE SEEN YOU SOMEWHERE ELSE—

MIMI

DO YOU GO TO THE CAT SCRATCH CLUB
THAT'S WHERE I WORK—I DANCE—HELP ME LOOK

ROGER

YES!
THEY USED TO TIE YOU UP—

MIMI

IT'S A LIVING

(MIMI douses the flame again.)

ROGER

I DIDN'T RECOGNIZE YOU
WITHOUT THE HANDCUFFS

MIMI

WE COULD LIGHT THE CANDLE
OH WON'T YOU LIGHT THE CANDLE?

(ROGER lights it again.)

ROGER

WHY DON'T YOU FORGET THAT STUFF
YOU LOOK LIKE YOU'RE SIXTEEN

MIMI

I'M NINETEEN—BUT I'M OLD FOR MY AGE
I'M JUST BORN TO BE BAD

ROGER

I ONCE WAS BORN TO BE BAD
I USED TO SHIVER LIKE THAT

MIMI

I HAVE NO HEAT—I TOLD YOU

ROGER

I USED TO SWEAT

MIMI

I GOT A COLD

> **ROGER**
> UH-HUH
> I USED TO BE A JUNKIE

> **MIMI**
> BUT NOW AND THEN I LIKE TO—

> **ROGER**
> UH-HUH

> **MIMI**
> FEEL GOOD

> **ROGER**
> HERE IT—UM—

(ROGER stoops and picks up a small object: MIMI's stash.)

> **MIMI**
> WHAT'S THAT?

> **ROGER**
> CANDY-BAR WRAPPER

(ROGER puts it behind his back and into his back pocket.)

> **MIMI**
> WE COULD LIGHT THE CANDLE

(ROGER discreetly blows out the candle.)

> **MIMI**
> WHAT'D YOU DO WITH MY CANDLE?

> **ROGER**
> THAT WAS MY LAST MATCH

> **MIMI**
> OUR EYES'LL ADJUST. THANK GOD FOR THE MOON

ROGER

MAYBE IT'S NOT THE MOON AT ALL
I HEAR SPIKE LEE'S SHOOTING DOWN THE STREET

MIMI

BAH HUMBUG . . . BAH HUMBUG

(MIMI places her hand under his, pretending to do it by mistake.)

ROGER

COLD HANDS

MIMI

YOURS TOO.
BIG. LIKE MY FATHER'S
YOU WANNA DANCE?

ROGER

WITH YOU?

MIMI

NO—WITH MY FATHER

ROGER

I'M ROGER

MIMI

THEY CALL ME
THEY CALL ME MIMI

(MIMI goes to him, arms around him. She reaches into his pocket, nabs the stash and sexily exits.)

9. Voice Mail #2

Joanne's loft

(In blackout another phone rings. We see MAUREEN in silhouette.)

MAUREEN
Hi. You've reached Maureen and Joanne. Leave a message and don't forget *Over the Moon*—my performance, protesting the eviction of the homeless (and artists) from the 11th Street lot. Tonight at midnight in the lot between A and B. Party at Life Cafe to follow. *(Beeep!)*

MR. JEFFERSON
WELL, JOANNE—WE'RE OFF
I TRIED YOU AT THE OFFICE
AND THEY SAID YOU'RE STAGE-MANAGING OR SOMETHING

MRS. JEFFERSON
REMIND HER THAT THOSE UNWED MOTHERS IN HARLEM
NEED HER LEGAL HELP, TOO

MR. JEFFERSON
CALL DAISY FOR OUR ITINERARY OR ALFRED AT POUND RIDGE
OR EILEEN AT THE STATE DEPARTMENT IN A PINCH
WE'LL BE AT THE SPA FOR NEW YEAR'S
UNLESS THE SENATOR CHANGES HIS MIND

MRS. JEFFERSON
THE HEARINGS

MR. JEFFERSON
OH YES—KITTEN
MUMMY'S CONFIRMATION HEARING BEGINS ON THE TENTH
WE'LL NEED YOU—ALONE—BY THE SIXTH

MRS. JEFFERSON
HAROLD!

                    MR. JEFFERSON
YOU HEAR THAT?
IT'S THREE WEEKS AWAY
AND SHE'S ALREADY NERVOUS

                    MRS. JEFFERSON
I AM NOT!

                    MR. JEFFERSON
FOR MUMMY'S SAKE, KITTEN
NO DOC MARTEN'S THIS TIME, AND WEAR A DRESS . . .
OH, AND, KITTEN—HAVE A MERRY—

                    MRS. JEFFERSON
AND A BRA!

10. Today 4 U

MARK and ROGER's loft

                    MARK
Enter Tom Collins, computer genius, teacher, vagabond anarchist
who ran naked through the Parthenon.

(COLLINS holds ANGEL's pickle tub, now filled with provisions.)

                    MARK and COLLINS
BUSTELO—MARLBORO
BANANA BY THE BUNCH
A BOX OF CAPTAIN CRUNCH WILL TASTE SO GOOD

                    COLLINS
AND FIREWOOD

                    MARK
LOOK—IT'S SANTA CLAUS

COLLINS
HOLD YOUR APPLAUSE

ROGER
OH HI

COLLINS
"OH HI" AFTER SEVEN MONTHS?

ROGER
SORRY

COLLINS
THIS BOY COULD USE SOME STOLI

COLLINS, MARK, and ROGER
OH HOLY NIGHT

ROGER
YOU STRUCK GOLD AT MIT?

COLLINS
THEY EXPELLED ME FOR MY THEORY OF ACTUAL REALITY
WHICH I'LL SOON IMPART
TO THE COUCH POTATOES AT NEW YORK UNIVERSITY
STILL HAVEN'T LEFT THE HOUSE?

ROGER
I WAS WAITING FOR YOU DON'T YOU KNOW?

COLLINS
WELL, TONIGHT'S THE NIGHT
COME TO THE LIFE CAFE AFTER MAUREEN'S SHOW

ROGER
NO FLOW

COLLINS

GENTLEMEN, OUR BENEFACTOR ON THIS CHRISTMAS EVE
WHOSE CHARITY IS ONLY MATCHED BY TALENT, I BELIEVE
A NEW MEMBER OF THE ALPHABET CITY AVANT-GARDE
ANGEL DUMOTT SCHUNARD!

(ANGEL sashays in. He's gorgeously done up in Santa drag, with a
fan of twenty-dollar bills in each hand.)

ANGEL

TODAY FOR YOU—TOMORROW FOR ME
TODAY FOR YOU—TOMORROW FOR ME

COLLINS

AND YOU SHOULD HEAR HER BEAT!

ROGER

YOU EARNED THIS ON THE STREET?

ANGEL

IT WAS MY LUCKY DAY TODAY ON AVENUE A
WHEN A LADY IN A LIMOUSINE DROVE MY WAY
SHE SAID, "DAHLING—BE A DEAR—HAVEN'T SLEPT IN A YEAR
I NEED YOUR HELP TO MAKE MY NEIGHBOR'S YAPPY DOG
DISAPPEAR"
"THIS AKITA—EVITA—JUST WON'T SHUT UP
I BELIEVE IF YOU PLAY NONSTOP THAT PUP
WILL BREATH ITS VERY LAST HIGH-STRUNG BREATH
I'M CERTAIN THAT CUR WILL BARK ITSELF TO DEATH"

TODAY FOR YOU—TOMORROW FOR ME
TODAY FOR YOU—TOMORROW FOR ME

WE AGREED ON A FEE—A THOUSAND DOLLAR GUARANTEE
TAX-FREE—AND A BONUS IF I TRIM HER TREE
NOW WHO COULD FORETELL THAT IT WOULD GO SO WELL
BUT SURE AS I AM HERE THAT DOG IS NOW IN DOGGY HELL

AFTER AN HOUR—EVITA—IN ALL HER GLORY
ON THE WINDOW LEDGE OF HER 23RD STORY

LIKE THELMA AND LOUISE DID WHEN THEY GOT THE BLUES
SWAN-DOVE INTO THE COURTYARD OF THE GRACIE MEWS

TODAY FOR YOU—TOMORROW FOR ME
TODAY FOR YOU—TOMORROW FOR ME

(ANGEL does a fantabulous drum solo and dance solo.)

THEN BACK TO THE STREET WHERE I MET MY SWEET
WHERE HE WAS MOANING AND GROANING ON THE COLD
CONCRETE
THE NURSE TOOK HIM HOME FOR SOME MERCUROCHROME
AND I DRESSED HIS WOUNDS AND GOT HIM BACK ON HIS FEET

SING IT
TODAY FOR YOU—TOMORROW FOR ME
TODAY FOR YOU—TOMORROW FOR ME
TODAY FOR YOU—TOMORROW FOR ME
TODAY FOR YOU—TOMORROW FOR ME

11. You'll See

(BENNY enters.)

BENNY
JOY TO THE WORLD—HEY, YOU BUM—YEAH, YOU, MOVE OVER
GET YOUR ASS OFF THAT RANGE ROVER

MARK
That attitude toward the homeless is exactly what Maureen is
protesting tonight.
> (to audience, holding camera up to BENNY)
Close up: Benjamin Coffin the Third, our ex-roommate, who married
Alison Grey, of the Westport Greys, then bought the building
and the lot next door from his father-in-law in hopes of starting a
cyberstudio.

BENNY

MAUREEN IS PROTESTING
LOSING HER PERFORMANCE SPACE
NOT MY ATTITUDE

ROGER

WHAT HAPPENED TO BENNY
WHAT HAPPENED TO HIS HEART
AND THE IDEALS HE ONCE PURSUED

BENNY

ANY OWNER OF THE LOT NEXT DOOR
HAS THE RIGHT TO DO WITH IT AS HE PLEASES

COLLINS

HAPPY BIRTHDAY, JESUS!

BENNY

THE RENT

MARK

YOU'RE WASTING YOUR TIME

BENNY

WE'RE BROKE

MARK

AND YOU BROKE YOUR WORD—THIS IS ABSURD

BENNY

THERE IS ONE WAY YOU WON'T HAVE TO PAY

ROGER

I KNEW IT!

BENNY

NEXT DOOR, THE HOME OF CYBERARTS, YOU SEE
AND NOW THAT THE BLOCK IS RE-ZONED
OUR DREAM CAN BECOME A REALITY

YOU'LL SEE, BOYS
YOU'LL SEE, BOYS
A STATE-OF-THE-ART DIGITAL, VIRTUAL, INTERACTIVE STUDIO
I'LL FOREGO YOUR RENT AND ON PAPER GUARANTEE
THAT YOU CAN STAY HERE FOR FREE
IF YOU DO ME ONE SMALL FAVOR

MARK

WHAT?

BENNY

CONVINCE MAUREEN TO CANCEL HER PROTEST

MARK

WHY NOT JUST GET AN INJUNCTION AND CALL THE COPS?

BENNY

I DID, AND THEY'RE ON STANDBY
BUT MY INVESTORS WOULD RATHER
I HANDLE THIS QUIETLY

ROGER

YOU CAN'T QUIETLY WIPE OUT AN ENTIRE TENT CITY
THEN WATCH *IT'S A WONDERFUL LIFE* ON TV!

BENNY

YOU WANT TO PRODUCE FILMS AND WRITE SONGS?
YOU NEED SOMEWHERE TO DO IT!
IT'S WHAT WE USED TO DREAM ABOUT
THINK TWICE BEFORE YOU POOH-POOH IT

YOU'LL SEE, BOYS
YOU'LL SEE, BOYS

YOU'LL SEE—THE BEAUTY OF A STUDIO
THAT LETS US DO OUR WORK AND GET PAID
WITH CONDOS ON THE TOP
WHOSE RENT KEEPS OPEN OUR SHOP

JUST STOP HER PROTEST
AND YOU'LL HAVE IT MADE
YOU'LL SEE—OR YOU'LL PACK

(BENNY exits.)

ANGEL
THAT BOY COULD USE SOME PROZAC

ROGER
OR HEAVY DRUGS

MARK
OR GROUP HUGS

COLLINS
WHICH REMINDS ME—
WE HAVE A DETOUR TO MAKE TONIGHT
ANYONE WHO WANTS TO CAN COME ALONG

ANGEL
LIFE SUPPORT'S A GROUP FOR PEOPLE COPING WITH LIFE
WE DON'T HAVE TO STAY TOO LONG

MARK
FIRST I'VE GOT A PROTEST TO SAVE

ANGEL
ROGER?

ROGER
I'M NOT VERY MUCH COMPANY, YOU'LL FIND

MARK
BEHAVE!

ANGEL
HE'LL CATCH UP LATER—HE'S GOT OTHER THINGS ON HIS MIND
YOU'LL SEE, BOYS

                    MARK and COLLINS
WE'LL SEE, BOYS

                            ROGER
LET IT BE, BOYS

                            COLLINS
I LIKE BOYS

                            ANGEL
BOYS LIKE ME

                            ALL
WE'LL SEE

12. Tango: Maureen

The Lot

(JOANNE is reexamining the cable connections for the umpteenth time.)

                        MARK
AND SO—INTO THE ABYSS
THE LOT. WHERE A SMALL STAGE IS PARTIALLY-SET UP

                        JOANNE
"LINE IN . . ."
I WENT TO HARVARD FOR THIS . . .

                        MARK
CLOSE ON MARK'S NOSEDIVE

                        JOANNE
"LINE OUT . . ."

                        MARK
WILL HE GET OUT OF HERE ALIVE . . . ?

(JOANNE notices MARK approaching.)

JOANNE
MARK?

MARK
HI.

JOANNE
I TOLD HER NOT TO CALL YOU

MARK
THAT'S MAUREEN
BUT CAN I HELP SINCE I'M HERE?

JOANNE
I HIRED AN ENGINEER . . .

MARK
GREAT!
SO, NICE TO HAVE MET YOU

JOANNE
WAIT!
SHE'S THREE HOURS LATE
THE SAMPLES WON'T DELAY
BUT THE CABLE—

MARK
THERE'S ANOTHER WAY
SAY SOMETHING—ANYTHING

JOANNE
(into the mike)
TEST—ONE, TWO THREE . . .

MARK
ANYTHING BUT THAT

JOANNE
THIS IS WEIRD

MARK

IT'S WEIRD

JOANNE

VERY WEIRD

MARK

FUCKIN' WEIRD

JOANNE

I'M SO MAD
THAT I DON'T KNOW WHAT TO DO
FIGHTING WITH MICROPHONES
FREEZING DOWN TO MY BONES
AND TO TOP IT ALL OFF
I'M WITH YOU

MARK

FEEL LIKE GOING INSANE?
GOT A FIRE IN YOUR BRAIN?
AND YOU'RE THINKING OF DRINKING GASOLINE?

JOANNE

AS A MATTER OF FACT—

MARK

HONEY, I KNOW THIS ACT
IT'S CALLED THE TANGO MAUREEN

THE TANGO MAUREEN
IT'S A DARK, DIZZY
MERRY-GO-ROUND
AS SHE KEEPS YOU DANGLING

JOANNE

YOU'RE WRONG

MARK

YOUR HEART SHE IS MANGLING

JOANNE

IT'S DIFFERENT WITH ME

MARK

AND YOU TOSS AND YOU TURN
'CAUSE HER COLD EYES CAN BURN
YET YOU YEARN AND YOU CHURN AND REBOUND

JOANNE

I THINK I KNOW WHAT YOU MEAN

BOTH

THE TANGO MAUREEN

MARK

HAS SHE EVER
POUTED HER LIPS
AND CALLED YOU "POOKIE"?

JOANNE

NEVER

MARK

HAVE YOU EVER DOUBTED A KISS OR TWO?

JOANNE

THIS IS SPOOKY
DID YOU SWOON
WHEN SHE WALKED THROUGH THE DOOR?

MARK

EVERY TIME—SO BE CAUTIOUS

JOANNE

DID SHE MOON OVER OTHER BOYS—?

MARK

MORE THAN MOON—

JOANNE
I'M GETTING NAUSEOUS

(They begin to dance, with MARK leading.)

MARK
Where'd you learn to tango?

JOANNE
With the French Ambassador's daughter in her dorm room at Miss Porter's. And you?

MARK
With Nanette Himmelfarb, the rabbi's daughter, at the Scarsdale Jewish Community Center.

(They switch, and JOANNE leads.)

MARK
It's hard to do this backward.

JOANNE
You should try it in heels!
SHE CHEATED

MARK
SHE CHEATED

JOANNE
MAUREEN CHEATED

MARK
FUCKIN' CHEATED

JOANNE
I'M DEFEATED
I SHOULD GIVE UP RIGHT NOW

MARK
GOTTA LOOK ON THE BRIGHT SIDE
WITH ALL YOUR MIGHT

JOANNE
I'D FALL FOR HER STILL ANYHOW

BOTH
WHEN YOU'RE DANCING HER DANCE
YOU DON'T STAND A CHANCE
HER GRIP OF ROMANCE
MAKES YOU FALL

MARK
SO YOU THINK, "MIGHT AS WELL"

JOANNE
"DANCE A TANGO TO HELL"

BOTH
"AT LEAST I'LL HAVE TANGOED AT ALL"
THE TANGO MAUREEN
GOTTA DANCE 'TIL YOUR DIVA IS THROUGH
YOU PRETEND TO BELIEVE HER 'CAUSE IN THE END—YOU CAN'T
LEAVE HER

BUT THE END IT WILL COME
STILL YOU HAVE TO PLAY DUMB
'TIL YOU'RE GLUM AND YOU BUM
AND TURN BLUE

MARK
WHY DO WE LOVE WHEN SHE'S MEAN?

JOANNE
AND SHE CAN BE SO OBSCENE

MARK
TRY THE MIKE

JOANNE
(The word echoes in digital delay land.)
MY MAUREEN (EEN, EEN, EEN. . .)

                              MARK
PATCHED

                             JOANNE
THANKS

                              MARK
YOU KNOW—I FEEL GREAT NOW!

                             JOANNE
I FEEL LOUSY

(The pay phone rings. MARK hands it to JOANNE.)

                             JOANNE
HI, HONEY, WE'RE . . .
POOKIE?
YOU NEVER CALLED ME POOKIE
FORGET IT
WE'RE PATCHED

(Joanne hangs up, looks at MARK.)

                              BOTH
THE TANGO MAUREEN!

13. Life Support

"Life Support" Group

(PAUL, the support group leader, sits on the downstage railing on
the right above, facing upstage. GORDON, one of the members of
the group, is standing downstage left, facing the audience. As they
enter they introduce themselves and form a semi-circle.)

(Note: the names of the HIV support group members should change
every night and should honor actual friends of the company who
have died of AIDS.)

STEVE

Steve.

GORDON

Gordon.

ALI

Ali.

PAM

Pam.

SUE

Sue.

ANGEL

Hi, I'm Angel.

COLLINS

Tom. Collins.

PAUL

I'm Paul. Let's begin.

ALL

THERE'S ONLY US
THERE'S ONLY THIS . . .

(MARK noisily enters.)

MARK

SORRY . . . EXCUSE ME . . . OOPS

PAUL

AND YOU ARE?

MARK

OH—I'M NOT—
I'M JUST HERE TO—
I DON'T HAVE—

I'M HERE WITH—
UM—MARK
MARK—I'm Mark.
WELL—THIS IS QUITE AN OPERATION

PAUL

SIT DOWN, MARK
WE'LL CONTINUE THE AFFIRMATION

ALL

FORGET REGRET, OR LIFE IS YOURS TO MISS

GORDON

EXCUSE ME, PAUL—I'M HAVING A PROBLEM WITH THIS
THIS CREDO—
MY T-CELLS ARE LOW—
I REGRET THAT NEWS, OKAY?

PAUL

ALL RIGHT
BUT, GORDON—HOW DO YOU FEEL TODAY?

GORDON

WHAT DO YOU MEAN?

PAUL

HOW DO YOU FEEL TODAY?

GORDON

OKAY

PAUL

IS THAT ALL?

GORDON

BEST I'VE FELT ALL YEAR

PAUL

THEN WHY CHOOSE FEAR?

GORDON

I'M A NEW YORKER!
FEAR'S MY LIFE!
LOOK—I FIND SOME OF WHAT YOU TEACH SUSPECT
BECAUSE I'M USED TO RELYING ON INTELLECT
BUT I TRY TO OPEN UP TO WHAT I DON'T KNOW

GORDON and ROGER
(who sings from his loft)
BECAUSE REASON SAYS I SHOULD HAVE DIED THREE YEARS AGO

ALL

NO OTHER ROAD
NO OTHER WAY
NO DAY BUT TODAY

14. Out Tonight

Mimi's apartment

MIMI

WHAT'S THE TIME?
WELL, IT'S GOTTA BE CLOSE TO MIDNIGHT
MY BODY'S TALKING TO ME
IT SAYS, "TIME FOR DANGER"

IT SAYS, "I WANNA COMMIT A CRIME
WANNA BE THE CAUSE OF A FIGHT
WANNA PUT ON A TIGHT SKIRT AND FLIRT WITH A STRANGER"

I'VE HAD A KNACK FROM WAY BACK
AT BREAKING THE RULES ONCE I LEARN THE GAMES
GET UP—LIFE'S TOO QUICK

I KNOW SOMEPLACE SICK
WHERE THIS CHICK'LL DANCE IN THE FLAMES
WE DON'T NEED ANY MONEY
I ALWAYS GET IN FOR FREE

YOU CAN GET IN TOO
IF YOU GET IN WITH ME

LET'S GO OUT TONIGHT
I HAVE TO GO OUT TONIGHT
YOU WANNA PLAY?
LET'S RUN AWAY
WE WON'T BE BACK
BEFORE IT'S CHRISTMAS DAY
TAKE ME OUT TONIGHT (MEOW)

WHEN I GET A WINK FROM THE DOORMAN
DO YOU KNOW HOW LUCKY YOU'LL BE?
THAT YOU'RE ON LINE WITH THE FELINE OF AVENUE B

LET'S GO OUT TONIGHT
I HAVE TO GO OUT TONIGHT
YOU WANNA PROWL
BE MY NIGHT OWL?
WELL, TAKE MY HAND
WE'RE GONNA HOWL
OUT TONIGHT

IN THE EVENING I'VE GOT TO ROAM
CAN'T SLEEP IN THE CITY OF NEON AND CHROME
FEELS TOO DAMN MUCH LIKE HOME
WHEN THE SPANISH BABIES CRY

SO LET'S FIND BAR
SO DARK WE FORGET WHO WE ARE
WHERE ALL THE SCARS FROM THE
NEVERS AND MAYBES DIE

LET'S GO OUT TONIGHT
HAVE TO GO OUT TONIGHT
YOU'RE SWEET
WANNA HIT THE STREET?
WANNA WAIL AT THE MOON LIKE A CAT IN HEAT?
JUST TAKE ME OUT TONIGHT

(MIMI makes her way to ROGER's door and ends the song in front of him.)

PLEASE TAKE ME OUT TONIGHT
DON'T FORSAKE ME—OUT TONIGHT
I'LL LET YOU MAKE ME—OUT TONIGHT
TONIGHT—TONIGHT—TONIGHT

15. Another Day

The loft

(MIMI plants a huge kiss on ROGER. He recoils.)

ROGER

WHO DO YOU THINK YOU ARE?
BARGING IN ON ME AND MY GUITAR
LITTLE GIRL—HEY
THE DOOR IS THAT WAY
YOU BETTER GO, YOU KNOW
THE FIRE'S OUT ANYWAY

TAKE YOUR POWDER—TAKE YOUR CANDLE
YOUR SWEET WHISPER
I JUST CAN'T HANDLE

WELL, TAKE YOUR HAIR IN THE MOONLIGHT
YOUR BROWN EYES—GOODBYE, GOODNIGHT

I SHOULD TELL YOU, I SHOULD TELL YOU
I SHOULD TELL YOU, I SHOULD—NO!

ANOTHER TIME—ANOTHER PLACE
OUR TEMPERATURES WOULD CLIMB
THERE'D BE A LONG EMBRACE
WE'D DO ANOTHER DANCE
IT'D BE ANOTHER PLAY
LOOKING FOR ROMANCE?

COME BACK ANOTHER DAY
ANOTHER DAY

MIMI

THE HEART MAY FREEZE OR IT CAN BURN
THE PAIN WILL EASE IF I CAN LEARN
THERE IS NO FUTURE
THERE IS NO PAST
I LIVE THIS MOMENT
AS MY LAST

THERE'S ONLY US
THERE'S ONLY THIS
FORGET REGRET
OR LIFE IS YOURS TO MISS
NO OTHER ROAD
NO OTHER WAY
NO DAY BUT TODAY

ROGER

EXCUSE ME IF I'M OFF TRACK
BUT IF YOU'RE SO WISE
THEN TELL ME—WHY DO YOU NEED SMACK?

TAKE YOUR NEEDLE
TAKE YOUR FANCY PRAYER
AND DON'T FORGET
GET THE MOONLIGHT OUT OF YOUR HAIR
LONG AGO—YOU MIGHT'VE LIT UP MY HEART
BUT THE FIRE'S DEAD—AIN'T NEVER GONNA START

ANOTHER TIME—ANOTHER PLACE
THE WORDS WOULD ONLY RHYME
WE'D BE IN OUTER SPACE
IT'D BE ANOTHER SONG
WE'D SING ANOTHER WAY
YOU WANNA PROVE ME WRONG?
COME BACK ANOTHER DAY
ANOTHER DAY

MIMI

THERE'S ONLY YES
ONLY TONIGHT
WE MUST LET GO
TO KNOW WHAT'S RIGHT
NO OTHER COURSE
NO OTHER WAY
NO DAY BUT TODAY

(Lights slowly fade up on the Life Support group.)

MIMI AND OTHERS	ROGER
I CAN'T CONTROL	CONTROL YOUR TEMPER
MY DESTINY	SHE DOESN'T SEE
I TRUST MY SOUL	WHO SAY'S THAT
	THERE'S A SOUL?
MY ONLY GOAL	
IS JUST—TO BE	JUST LET ME BE

ALL	
THERE'S ONLY NOW	WHO DO YOU THINK YOU ARE?
THERE'S ONLY HERE	
GIVE IN TO LOVE	BARGING IN ON ME AND MY GUITAR
OR LIVE IN FEAR	
NO OTHER PATH	LITTLE GIRL, HEY
NO OTHER WAY	
NO DAY BUT TODAY	THE DOOR IS THAT WAY
	THE FIRE'S OUT ANYWAY
NO DAY BUT TODAY	TAKE THE POWDER
	TAKE THE CANDLE
NO DAY BUT TODAY	TAKE YOUR BROWN EYES
	YOUR PRETTY SMILE
	YOUR SILHOUETTE
NO DAY BUT TODAY	ANOTHER TIME, ANOTHER PLACE
	ANOTHER RHYME, A WARM EMBRACE
NO DAY BUT TODAY	ANOTHER DANCE, ANOTHER WAY
	ANOTHER CHANCE, ANOTHER DAY
NO DAY BUT TODAY	

(MIMI and the Life Support group exit. One person, STEVE, stays at
stage right, above.)

16. Will I?

Various locations

ROGER
I'M WRITING ONE GREAT SONG BEFORE I . . .

STEVE
WILL I LOSE MY DIGNITY
WILL SOMEONE CARE
WILL I WAKE TOMORROW
FROM THIS NIGHTMARE?

GROUP #1
WILL I LOSE MY DIGNITY
WILL SOMEONE CARE
WILL I WAKE TOMORROW
FROM THIS NIGHTMARE?

GROUP #2
WILL I LOSE MY DIGNITY
WILL SOMEONE CARE
WILL I WAKE TOMORROW
FROM THIS NIGHTMARE?

GROUP #3
WILL I LOSE MY DIGNITY
WILL SOMEONE CARE
WILL I WAKE TOMORROW
FROM THIS NIGHTMARE?

GROUP #4
WILL I LOSE MY DIGNITY
WILL SOMEONE CARE
WILL I WAKE TOMORROW
FROM THIS NIGHTMARE?

(ROGER puts on his coat and exits loft.)

17. X-Mo Bells #2/Bummer

On the street

THREE HOMELESS PEOPLE
CHRISTMAS BELLS ARE RINGING
CHRISTMAS BELLS ARE RINGING
CHRISTMAS BELLS ARE RINGING—
OUT OF TOWN
SANTA FE

SQUEEGEEMAN
HONEST LIVING, MAN!

(SQEEGEEMAN recoils as if he's almost been run over by a car.)

FELIZ NAVIDAD!

(Three POLICE OFFICERS—in full riot gear—enter and approach sleeping BLANKET PERSON. The FIRST OFFICER pokes her with a nightstick.)

HOMELESS PERSON
EVENING, OFFICERS

(Without answering, the FIRST OFFICER raises his nightstick again.)

MARK
(pointing his camera)
SMILE FOR TED KOPPEL, OFFICER MARTIN!

(The FIRST OFFICER lowers his stick.)

HOMELESS PERSON
AND A MERRY CHRISTMAS TO YOUR FAMILY

POLICE OFFICERS
RIGHT!

(The POLICE OFFICERS exit. MARK films BLANKET PERSON.)

BLANKET PERSON
(to MARK)
WHO THE FUCK DO YOU THINK YOU ARE?
I DON'T NEED NO GODDAMN HELP
FROM SOME BLEEDING HEART CAMERAMAN
MY LIFE'S NOT FOR YOU TO
MAKE A NAME FOR YOURSELF ON!

ANGEL
EASY, SUGAR, EASY
HE WAS JUST TRYING TO—

BLANKET PERSON
JUST TRYING TO USE ME TO KILL HIS GUILT
IT'S NOT THAT KIND OF MOVIE, HONEY
LET'S GO—THIS LOT IS FULL, OF
MOTHERFUCKING ARTISTS
HEY, ARTISTS
GOTTA DOLLAR?
I THOUGHT NOT

(BLANKET PERSON crosses to downstage left with another
HOMELESS PERSON.)

18. Santa Fe

ANGEL
NEW YORK CITY—

MARK
UH-HUH

ANGEL
CENTER OF THE UNIVERSE

COLLINS

SING IT, GIRL—

ANGEL

TIMES ARE SHITTY
BUT I'M PRETTY SURE THEY CAN'T GET WORSE

MARK

I HEAR YOU

ANGEL

IT'S A COMFORT TO KNOW
WHEN YOU'RE SINGING THE HIT-THE-ROAD BLUES
THAT ANYWHERE ELSE YOU COULD POSSIBLY GO
AFTER NEW YORK'D BE A PLEASURE CRUISE

COLLINS

NOW YOU'RE TALKING
WELL, I'M THWARTED BY A METAPHYSIC PUZZLE
AND I'M SICK OF GRADING PAPERS - THAT I KNOW
AND I'M SHOUTING IN MY SLEEP, I NEED A MUZZLE
ALL THIS MISERY PAYS NO SALARY, SO
LET'S OPEN UP A RESTAURANT
IN SANTA FE
OH SUNNY SANTA FE WOULD BE NICE
WE'LL OPEN UP A RESTAURANT IN SANTA FE
AND LEAVE THIS TO THE ROACHES AND MICE
OH—OH

ALL

OH—

ANGEL

YOU TEACH?

COLLINS

I TEACH—COMPUTER-AGE PHILOSOPHY
BUT MY STUDENTS WOULD RATHER WATCH TV

ANGEL

AMERICA

ALL

AMERICA !

COLLINS

YOU'RE A SENSITIVE AESTHETE
BRUSH THE SAUCE ONTO THE MEAT
YOU COULD MAKE THE MENU SPARKLE WITH RHYME
YOU COULD DRUM A GENTLE DRUM
I COULD SEAT GUESTS AS THEY COME
CHATTING NOT ABOUT HEIDEGGER, BUT WINE!
   (with HOMELESS PEOPLE in the shadows)
LET'S OPEN UP A RESTAURANT IN SANTA FE

ALL

SANTA FE

COLLINS

OUR LABORS WOULD REAP
FINANCIAL GAINS

ALL

GAINS, GAINS, GAINS

COLLINS

WE'LL OPEN UP A RESTAURANT
IN SANTA FE

ALL

SANTA FE

COLLINS

AND SAVE FROM DEVASTATION OUR BRAINS

HOMELESS PEOPLE

SAVE OUR BRAINS

COLLINS
WE'LL PACK UP ALL OUR JUNK AND FLY SO FAR AWAY
DEVOTE OURSELVES TO PROJECTS THAT SELL
WE'LL OPEN UP A RESTAURANT IN SANTA FE

ALL
SANTA FE
FORGET THIS COLD BOHEMIAN HELL
OH—

ALL
OH—

COLLINS
DO YOU KNOW THE WAY TO SANTA FE?
YOU KNOW, TUMBLEWEEDS . . . PRAIRIE DOGS . . .
YEAH

19. I'll Cover You

The street

MARK
I'll meet you at the show. I'll try and convince Roger to go.

(MARK exits.)

ANGEL
Alone at last.

COLLINS
He'll be back—I guarantee.

ANGEL
I've been hearing violins all night.

COLLINS
Anything to do with me? Are we a thing?

ANGEL

Darling—we're everything.
LIVE IN MY HOUSE
I'LL BE YOUR SHELTER
JUST PAY ME BACK
WITH ONE THOUSAND KISSES
BE MY LOVER—I'LL COVER YOU

COLLINS

OPEN YOUR DOOR
I'LL BE YOUR TENANT
DON'T GOT MUCH BAGGAGE
TO LAY AT YOUR FEET
BUT SWEET KISSES I'VE GOT TO SPARE
I'LL BE THERE—I'LL COVER YOU

BOTH

I THINK THEY MEANT IT
WHEN THEY SAID THAT YOU CAN'T BUY LOVE
NOW I KNOW YOU CAN RENT IT
A NEW LEASE YOU ARE, MY LOVE,
ON LIFE—BE MY LIFE

(COLLINS and ANGEL do a short dance.)

JUST SLIP ME ON
I'LL BE YOUR BLANKET
WHEREVER—WHATEVER—I'LL BE YOUR COAT

ANGEL

YOU'LL BE MY KING
AND I'LL BE YOUR CASTLE

COLLINS

NO, YOU'LL BE MY QUEEN
AND I'LL BE YOUR MOAT

BOTH

I THINK THEY MEANT IT
WHEN THEY SAID YOU CAN'T BUY LOVE
NOW I KNOW YOU CAN RENT IT

A NEW LEASE YOU ARE, MY LOVE
ON LIFE
ALL MY LIFE
I'VE LONGED TO DISCOVER
SOMETHING AS TRUE AS THIS IS

COLLINS
SO WITH A THOUSAND
SWEET KISSES
I'LL COVER YOU

WITH A THOUSAND SWEET
KISSES I'LL COVER YOU

WHEN YOU'RE WORN OUT AND
TIRED

WHEN YOUR HEART HAS EXPIRED

ANGEL

IF YOU'RE COLD AND YOU'RE
LONELY

YOU GOT ONE NICKEL ONLY

WITH A THOUSAND SWEET
KISSES I'LL COVER YOU

WITH A THOUSAND SWEET
KISSES I'LL COVER YOU

BOTH
OH LOVER, I'LL COVER YOU
OH LOVER, I'LL COVER YOU

20. We're Okay

At the pay phone

JOANNE
(on her cellular phone)
STEVE—JOANNE
THE MURGET CASE?
A DISMISSAL!
GREAT WORK, COUNSELOR

(The pay phone rings. JOANNE answers it.)

WE'RE OKAY
HONEYBEAR—WAIT!
I'M ON THE OTHER PHONE
YES, I HAVE THE COWBELL
WE'RE OKAY
                    (into the cellular phone)
SO TELL THEM WE'LL SUE
BUT A SETTLEMENT WILL DO
SEXUAL HARASSMENT—AND CIVIL RIGHTS, TOO
STEVE, YOU'RE GREAT
                    (into the pay phone)
NO, YOU CUT THE PAPER PLATE
DIDJA CHEAT ON MARK A LOT WOULD YOU SAY?
WE'RE OKAY
Honey, hold on . . .
                    (into the cellular phone)
Steve . . . hold on . . .

(JOANNE presses the call-waiting button on the cellular phone.)

HELLO?
DAD—YES
I BEEPED YOU
MAUREEN IS COMING TO MOTHER'S HEARING
WE'RE OKAY
                    (into the pay phone)
HONEYBEAR—WHAT? NEWT'S LESBIAN SISTER
I'LL TELL THEM
                    (into the cellular phone)
YOU HEARD?
                    (into the pay phone)
THEY HEARD
WE'RE OKAY
                    (into the cellular phone)
AND TO YOU, DAD

(JOANNE presses call-waiting as she says into the pay phone.)

OH—JILL IS THERE?
> (into the cellular phone)

STEVE, GOTTA GO—
> (into the pay phone)

JILL WITH THE SHORT BLACK HAIR?
THE CALVIN KLEIN MODEL?
> (into the cellular phone)

STEVE, GOTTA GO!
> (into the pay phone)

THE MODEL WHO LIVES IN PENTHOUSE A?
WE'RE
WE'RE OKAY
I'M ON MY WAY

21. Christmas Bells

Various locations, St. Mark's Place

FIVE HOMELESS PEOPLE
CHRISTMAS BELLS ARE RINGING
CHRISTMAS BELLS ARE RINGING
CHRISTMAS BELLS ARE RINGING
ON TV—AT SAKS

SQUEEGEEMAN
HONEST LIVING, HONEST LIVING
HONEST LIVING, HONEST LIVING
HONEST LIVING, HONEST LIVING

FIVE HOMELESS PEOPLE
CAN'T YOU SPARE A DIME OR TWO
HERE BUT FOR THE GRACE OF GOD GO YOU
YOU'LL BE MERRY
I'LL BE MERRY
THO MERRY AIN'T IN MY VOCABULARY

NO SLEIGH BELLS
NO SANTA CLAUS
NO YULE LOG
NO TINSEL
NO HOLLY
NO HEARTH
NO

SOLOIST
RUDOLPH THE RED NOSED REINDEER

ALL FIVE
RUDOLPH THE RED NOSED REINDEER
NO ROOM AT THE HOLIDAY INN—OH NO

(A few flakes of snow descend.)

AND IT'S BEGINNING TO SNOW

(The blank stage explodes into life! St. Mark's Place on Christmas Eve—an open air bazaar of color, noise, movement . . .)

VENDORS
HATS, BATS, SHOES, BOOZE
MOUNTAIN BIKES, POTPOURRI
LEATHER BAGS, GIRLIE MAGS
FORTY-FIVES, AZT

VENDOR #1
NO ONE'S BUYING
FEEL LIKE CRYING

ALL
NO ROOM AT THE HOLIDAY INN, OH NO
AND IT'S BEGINNING TO SNOW

(Lights up on one woman, showing off a collection of stolen coats to COLLINS and ANGEL.)

VENDOR #2

HOW ABOUT A FUR—
IN PERFECT SHAPE
OWNED BY AN MBA FROM UPTOWN

I GOT A TWEED
BROKEN IN BY A GREEDY
BROKER WHO WENT BROKE
AND THEN BROKE DOWN

COLLINS

YOU DON'T HAVE TO DO THIS

ANGEL

HUSH YOUR MOUTH, IT'S CHRISTMAS

COLLINS

I DO NOT DESERVE YOU, ANGEL

COLLINS	ANGEL
GIVE—GIVE	WAIT—WHAT'S ON
ALL YOU DO	THE FLOOR?
IS GIVE	LET'S SEE SOME MORE
GIVE ME SOME WAY TO SHOW	NO—NO—NO . . .
HOW YOU'VE TOUCHED ME SO	

ANGEL

KISS ME—IT'S BEGINNING TO SNOW

(Lights focus on MARK and ROGER on right above.)

MARK

. . . SHE SAID, "WOULD YOU LIGHT MY CANDLE"
AND SHE PUT ON A POUT
AND SHE WANTED YOU
TO TAKE HER OUT TONIGHT?

ROGER

RIGHT

MARK
SHE GOT YOU OUT!

ROGER
SHE WAS MORE THAN OKAY
BUT I PUSHED HER AWAY
IT WAS BAD—I GOT MAD
AND I HAD TO GET HER OUT OF MY SIGHT

MARK
WAIT, WAIT, WAIT—YOU SAID SHE WAS SWEET

ROGER
LET'S GO EAT—I'LL JUST GET FAT
IT'S THE ONE VICE LEFT—WHEN YOU'RE DEAD MEAT

(MIMI has entered looking furtively for THE MAN.)

ROGER
THERE—THAT'S HER

MARK
MAUREEN?

ROGER
MIMI!

MARK
WHOA!

ROGER
I SHOULD GO

BOTH
HEY—IT'S BEGINNING TO SNOW

(The POLICE OFFICERS, in riot gear, enter above.)

POLICE OFFICERS
I'M DREAMING OF A WHITE, RIGHT CHRISTMAS

(POLICE OFFICERS exit.)

MIMI and JUNKIES
FOLLOW THE MAN—FOLLOW THE MAN
WITH HIS POCKETS FULL OF THE JAM
FOLLOW THE MAN—FOLLOW THE MAN
HELP ME OUT, DADDY
IF YOU CAN
GOT ANY D, MAN?

THE MAN
I'M COOL

MIMI and JUNKIES
GOT ANY C, MAN?

THE MAN
I'M COOL

MIMI and JUNKIES
GOT ANY X
ANY SMACK
ANY HORSE
ANY JUGIE BOOGIE, BOY
ANY BLOW?

(ROGER pulls MIMI aside.)

ROGER
HEY

MIMI
HEY

ROGER
I JUST WANT TO SAY
I'M SORRY FOR THE WAY—

MIMI

FORGET IT

ROGER

I BLEW UP
CAN I MAKE IT UP TO YOU?

MIMI

HOW?

ROGER

DINNER PARTY?

MIMI

THAT'LL DO

THE MAN

HEY, LOVER BOY—CUTIE PIE
YOU STEAL MY CLIENT—YOU DIE

ROGER

YOU DIDN'T MISS ME—YOU WON'T MISS HER
YOU'LL NEVER LACK FOR CUSTOMERS

JUNKIES

I'M WILLIN'
I'M ILLIN'
I GOTTA GET MY SICKNESS OFF
GOTTA RUN, GOTTA RIDE
GOTTA GUN, GOTTA HIDE—GOTTA GO

THE MAN

AND IT'S BEGINNING TO SNOW

(BENNY enters, talking on his cellular phone.)

BENNY

WE'RE OUT OF LUCK, ALISON—
THE PROTEST IS ON.

COAT VENDOR
L.L. BEAN,
GEOFFREY BEENE,
BURBERRY ZIP-OUT LINING

JUNKIES
GOT ANY C, MAN?
GOT ANY D, MAN?
GOT ANY B, MAN
GOT ANY CRACK?
GOT ANY X?

SQUEEGEEMAN
HONEST LIVING—

ROGER
MARK, THIS IS MIMI—

MARK and MIMI
HI

ROGER
SHE'LL BE DINNING—WITH US

COAT VENDOR
HERE'S A NEW ARRIVAL

THE MAN
THAT IS AN OUNCE

VENDORS
HATS, DATS, BATS

COLLINS
THAT'S MY COAT!

COAT VENDOR
WE GIVE DISCOUNTS

MARK
I THINK WE'VE MET

ANGEL
LET'S GET A BETTER ONE

COLLINS

IT'S A SHAM

MIMI

THAT'S WHAT HE SAID

THE MAN

I SAID IT'S A GRAM!

COLLINS

BUT SHE'S A THIEF!

ANGEL

BUT SHE BOUGHT US TOGETHER

BENNY

WHICH INVESTOR IS COMING??

COLLINS

I'LL TAKE THE LEATHER

BENNY

YOUR FATHER?—DAMN!

(The following is sung simultaneously.)

HOMELESS and VENDORS

CHRISTMAS BELLS ARE SWINGING
CHRISTMAS BELLS ARE RINGING
CHRISTMAS BELLS ARE SINGING
IN MY DREAMS—NEXT YEAR
ONCE YOU DONATE YOU CAN GO
CELEBRATE IN TUCKAHOE
YOU'LL FEEL CHERRY
I'LL FEEL CHEERY
THO' I DON'T REALLY KNOW THAT THEORY
NO BATHROBE
NO STEUBEN GLASS
NO CAPPUCCINO MAKERS

NO PEARLS, NO DIAMONDS
NO "CHESTNUTS ROASTING ON AN OPEN FIRE"
CHESTNUTS ROASTING ON AN OPEN FIRE
NO ROOM AT THE HOLIDAY INN, OH NO—

POLICE OFFICERS

I'M DREAMING OF A RIGHT CHRISTMAS
JUST LIKE THE ONES I USED TO KNOW
JINGLE BELLS—PRISON CELLS

FA LA LA LA—FA LA LA LA
YOU HAVE THE RIGHT TO REMAIN
SILENT NIGHT HOLY NIGHT

FALL ON YOUR KNEES OH NIGHT DIVINE
YOU'LL DO SOME TIME
FA LA LA LA LA
FA LA LA LA LA

JUNKIES

GOT ANY C, MAN? GOT ANY D, MAN? GOT ANY B, MAN
GOT ANY X?—CRACK?

I'M WILLIN'—I'M ILLIN'
GOTTA GET MY SICKNESS OFF
C-D HELP ME
FOLLOW THE MAN—FOLLOW THE MAN
FOLLOW THE MAN
JUGIE BOOGIE—JUGIE BOOGIE

FOLLOW THE MAN—FOLLOW THE MAN
ANY CRACK ANY X ANY JUGIE BOOGIE BOY
ANY BLOW ANY X ANY JUGIE BOOGIE BOY
GOT ANY D, MAN, GOT ANY C, MAN
GOT ANY CRACK, ANY X, ANY JUGIE BOOGIE?

COAT VENDOR

TWENTY-FIVE

RENT

ANGEL

FIFTEEN

COAT VENDOR

TWENTY-FIVE

ANGEL

FIFTEEN

COAT VENDOR

TWENTY-FIVE

ANGEL

FIFTEEN

COAT VENDOR

NO WAY
TWENTY-FOUR

ANGEL

FIFTEEN

COAT VENDOR

TWENTY-FOUR

ANGEL

FIFTEEN

COAT VENDOR

TWENTY-FOUR

ANGEL

FIFTEEN

COAT VENDOR

NOT TODAY
TWENTY-THREE

ANGEL

FIFTEEN

                    COAT VENDOR
TWENTY-THREE

                         ANGEL
FIFTEEN

                    COAT VENDOR
TWENTY-THREE

                         ANGEL
FIFTEEN—IT'S OLD

                    COAT VENDOR
TWENTY-TWO

                         ANGEL
FIFTEEN

                    COAT VENDOR
TWENTY-ONE

                         ANGEL
FIFTEEN

                    COAT VENDOR
SEVENTEEN

                         ANGEL
FIFTEEN

                    COAT VENDOR
FIFTEEN

              ANGEL and COAT VENDOR
SOLD!

MARK and ROGER

LET'S
GO TO
THE LOT—
MAUREEN'S PERFORMING

MIMI

WHO'S MAUREEN?

ROGER

HIS EX

MARK

BUT I AM OVER HER

ROGER

LET'S
NOT
HOLD HANDS YET

MIMI

IS THAT A WARNING?

ALL THREE

HE—YOU—I
JUST
NEED(S)
TO TAKE IT SLOW
I SHOULD TELL YOU I SHOULD TELL YOU
I SHOULD TELL YOU I SHOULD TELL YOU
I SHOULD TELL YOU I . . .

ALL

AND IT'S BEGINNING TO
AND IT'S BEGINNING TO
AND IT'S BEGINNING TO—

(Lights blackout and we see a headlight come through the door.
As it reaches downstage, lights come up and reveal MAUREEN
down center.)

MAUREEN

Joanne, which way to the stage!

ALL

SNOW!!!

(Blackout.)

22. Over the Moon

The lot

MARK

Maureen's performance.

(Maureen stands in front of a microphone.)

MAUREEN

LAST NIGHT I HAD THIS DREAM. I FOUND MYSELF IN A DESERT
CALLED CYBERLAND. IT WAS HOT. MY CANTEEN HAD SPRUNG A
LEAK AND I WAS THIRSTY. OUT OF THE ABYSS WALKED A COW—
ELSIE. I ASKED IF SHE HAD ANYTHING TO DRINK. SHE SAID, "I'M
FORBIDDEN TO PRODUCE MILK. IN CYBERLAND, WE ONLY DRINK
DIET COKE."
(reverb: Coke, Coke, Coke)
SHE SAID, "ONLY THING TO DO IS JUMP OVER THE MOON.
THEY'VE CLOSED EVERYTHING REAL DOWN . . . LIKE BARNS,
TROUGHS, PERFORMANCE SPACES . . . AND REPLACED IT ALL
WITH LIES AND RULES AND VIRTUAL LIFE.
(reverb: life, life, life)
BUT THERE IS A WAY OUT . . ."

BACKUPS

LEAP OF FAITH LEAP OF FAITH
LEAP OF FAITH LEAP OF FAITH

MAUREEN
"ONLY THING TO DO IS JUMP OVER THE MOON
I GOTTA GET OUT OF HERE! IT'S LIKE I'M BEING TIED TO
THE HOOD OF A YELLOW RENTAL TRUCK, PACKED IN WITH
FERTILIZER AND FUEL OIL, PUSHED OVER A CLIFF BY A SUICIDAL
MICKEY MOUSE!—I'VE GOTTA FIND A WAY"

MAUREEN	BACKUPS
"TO JUMP OVER THE MOON	LEAP OF FAITH, ETC.
ONLY THING TO DO IS	
JUMP OVER THE MOON"	

MAUREEN
THEN A LITTLE BULLDOG ENTERED. HIS NAME (WE HAVE
LEARNED) WAS BENNY. AND ALTHOUGH HE ONCE HAD
PRINCIPLES, HE ABANDONED THEM TO LIVE AS A LAPDOG TO A
WEALTHY DAUGHTER OF THE REVOLUTION.

"THAT'S BULL,"HE SAID. "EVER SINCE THE CAT TOOK UP THE
FIDDLE, THAT COW'S BEEN JUMPY. AND THE DISH AND SPOON
WERE EVICTED FROM THE TABLE—AND ELOPED . . . SHE'S
HAD TROUBLE WITH THAT MILK AND THAT MOON EVER SINCE.
MAYBE IT'S A FEMALE THING, 'CAUSE WHO'D WANT TO LEAVE
CYBERLAND ANYWAY? . . . WALLS AIN'T SO BAD. THE DISH
AND SPOON FOR INSTANCE. THEY WERE DOWN ON THEIR
LUCK—KNOCKED ON MY DOGHOUSE DOOR. I SAID, 'NOT IN
MY BACKYARD, UTENSILS! GO BACK TO CHINA! THE ONLY WAY
OUT—IS UP.'" ELSIE WHISPERED TO ME, "A LEAP OF FAITH.
STILL THIRSTY?" SHE ASKED. PARCHED. "HAVE SOME MILK." I
LOWERED MYSELF BENEATH HER SWOLLEN UDDER AND SUCKED
THE SWEETEST MILK I'D EVER TASTED.

(MAUREEN makes a slurping, sucking sound.)

"CLIMB ON BOARD," SHE SAID. AND AS A HARVEST MOON ROSE
OVER CYBERLAND, WE REARED BACK AND SPRANG INTO A
GALLOP. LEAPING OUT OF ORBIT!

MAUREEN	BACKUPS
AWOKE SINGING	LEAP OF FAITH, ETC.

MAUREEN
AWOKE SINGING
ONLY THING TO DO
ONLY THING TO DO IS JUMP
ONLY THING TO DO IS JUMP OVER
THE MOON
ONLY THING TO DO IS JUMP OVER
THE MOON
OVER THE MOON—OVER THE
MOOOOOOOO
MOOOOOOOO
MOOOOOOOO
MOO WITH ME.

(MAUREEN encourages the audience to moo with her. She says, "C'mon, sir, moo with me," etc. The audience responds. When the "moos" reach a crescendo, she cuts them off with a big sweep of her arms.)

Thank you.

(Blackout)

23. La Vie Bohème

Life Cafe

(Downstage right, the PRINCIPALS are lined up and waiting to be seated. Down center is a large table. Down and to the right is a smaller table occupied by BENNY and MR. GREY. The RESTAURANT MAN tries to shoo our friends out.)

RESTAURANT MAN
NO, PLEASE, NO
NOT TONIGHT, PLEASE, NO
MISTER—CAN'T YOU GO—
NOT TONIGHT—CAN'T HAVE A SCENE

                    ROGER
WHAT?

                RESTAURANT MAN
GO, PLEASE GO—
YOU—HELLO, SIR—
I SAID NO
IMPORTANT CUSTOMER

                    MARK
WHAT AM I—JUST A BLUR?

                RESTAURANT MAN
YOU SIT ALL NIGHT—YOU NEVER BUY!

                    MARK
THAT'S A LIE—THAT'S A LIE
I HAD A TEA THE OTHER DAY

                RESTAURANT MAN
YOU COULDN'T PAY.

                    MARK
OH YEAH

                    COLLINS
BENJAMIN COFFIN THE THIRD—HERE?

                RESTAURANT MAN
OH NO!

                    ALL
WINE AND BEER!

                    MAUREEN
THE ENEMY OF AVENUE A
WE'LL STAY

(THEY sit.)

RESTAURANT MAN

OY VEY!

COLLINS

WHAT BRINGS THE MOGUL IN HIS OWN MIND TO THE LIFE CAFE?

BENNY

I WOULD LIKE TO PROPOSE A TOAST
TO MAUREEN'S NOBLE TRY
IT WENT WELL

MAUREEN

GO TO HELL

BENNY

WAS THE YUPPIE SCUM STOMPED
NOT COUNTING THE HOMELESS
HOW MANY TICKETS WEREN'T COMP'ED

ROGER

WHY DID MUFFY—

BENNY

ALISON

ROGER

MISS THE SHOW?

BENNY

THERE WAS A DEATH IN THE FAMILY
IF YOU MUST KNOW

ANGEL

WHO DIED?

BENNY

OUR AKITA

(A beat)

RENT

BENNY, MARK, ANGEL, and COLLINS
EVITA

BENNY
MIMI—I'M SURPRISED
A BRIGHT AND CHARMING GIRL LIKE YOU
HANGS OUT WITH THESE SLACKERS
(WHO DON'T ADHERE TO DEALS)

THEY MAKE FUN—YET I'M THE ONE
ATTEMPTING TO DO SOME GOOD
OR DO YOU REALLY WANT A NEIGHBORHOOD
WHERE PEOPLE PISS ON YOUR STOOP EVERY NIGHT?
BOHEMIA, BOHEMIA'S
A FALLACY IN YOUR HEAD
THIS IS CALCUTTA
BOHEMIA'S DEAD

(The BOHEMIANS immediately begin to enact a mock funeral, with MARK delivering a "eulogy.")

MARK
DEARLY BELOVED, WE GATHER HERE TO SAY OUR GOODBYES

COLLINS and ROGER
DIES IRAE—DIES ILLA
KYRIE ELEISON
YITGADAL V'YITKADASH, etc.

MARK
HERE SHE LIES
NO ONE KNEW HER WORTH
THE LATE GREAT DAUGHTER OF MOTHER EARTH
ON THIS NIGHT WHEN WE CELEBRATE THE BIRTH
IN THAT LITTLE TOWN OF BETHLEHEM
WE RAISE OUR GLASS—YOU BET YOUR ASS TO—

(MAUREEN slashes hers.)

LA VIE BOHÈME

ALL

LA VIE BOHÈME
LA VIE BOHÈME
LA VIE BOHÈME
LA VIE BOHÈME

MARK

TO DAYS OF INSPIRATION
PLAYING HOOKY, MAKING SOMETHING
OUT OF NOTHING, THE NEED
TO EXPRESS—
TO COMMUNICATE,
TO GOING AGAINST THE GRAIN,
GOING INSANE,
GOING MAD

TO LOVING TENSION, NO PENSION,
TO MORE THAN ONE DIMENSION,
TO STARVING FOR ATTENTION,
HATING CONVENTION, HATING   PRETENSION,
NOT TO MENTION OF COURSE,
HATING DEAR OLD MOM AND DAD
TO RIDING YOUR BIKE,
MIDDAY PAST THE THREE PIECE SUITS—
TO FRUITS—TO NO ABSOLUTES—
TO ABSOLUT—TO CHOICE—
TO THE *VILLAGE VOICE*—
TO ANY PASSING FAD

TO BEING AN US—FOR ONCE— . . .
INSTEAD OF A THEM—

ALL

LA VIE BOHÈME
LA VIE BOHÈME

(JOANNE enters.)

MAUREEN

IS THE EQUIPMENT IN A PYRAMID?

JOANNE

IT IS, MAUREEN

MAUREEN

THE MIXER DOESN'T HAVE A CASE
DON'T GIVE ME THAT FACE

(MAUREEN smacks JOANNE'S ass as she exits. MR. GREY reacts.)

MR. GREY

AHHEMM!

MAUREEN

HEY, MISTER—SHE'S MY SISTER

RESTAURANT MAN

SO THAT'S FIVE MISO SOUP, FOUR SEAWEED SALAD
THREE SOY BURGER DINNER, TWO TOFU DOG PLATTER
AND ONE PASTA WITH MEATLESS BALLS

A BOY

UGH

COLLINS

IT TASTES THE SAME

MIMI

IF YOU CLOSE YOUR EYES

RESTAURANT MAN

AND THIRTEEN ORDERS OF FRIES
IS THAT IT HERE?

ALL

WINE AND BEER!

MIMI and ANGEL

TO HAND-CRAFTED BEERS MADE IN LOCAL BREWERIES
TO YOGA, TO YOGURT, TO RICE AND BEANS AND CHEESE
TO LEATHER, TO DILDOS, TO CURRY VINDALOO
TO HUEVOS RANCHEROS AND MAYA ANGELOU

MAUREEN and COLLINS
EMOTION, DEVOTION, TO CAUSING A COMMOTION
CREATION, VACATION

MARK
MUCHO MASTURBATION

MAUREEN and COLLINS
COMPASSION, TO FASHION, TO PASSION WHEN IT'S NEW

COLLINS
TO SONTAG

ANGEL
TO SONDHEIM

FOUR PEOPLE
TO ANYTHING TABOO

COLLINS and ROGER
GINSBERG, DYLAN, CUNNINGHAM AND CAGE

COLLINS
LENNY BRUCE

ROGER
LANGSTON HUGHES

MAUREEN
TO THE STAGE

PERSON #1
TO UTA

PERSON #2
TO BUDDHA

PERSON #3
PABLO NERUDA, TOO

MARK and MIMI
WHY DOROTHY AND TOTO WENT OVER THE RAINBOW
TO BLOW OFF AUNTIE EM

ALL
LA VIE BOHÈME

(JOANNE returns.)

MAUREEN
AND WIPE THE SPEAKERS OFF BEFORE YOU PACK

JOANNE
YES, MAUREEN

MAUREEN
WELL—HURRY BACK

(MAUREEN and JOANNE kiss.)

MR. GREY
SISTERS?

MAUREEN
WE'RE CLOSE

(ANGEL jumps on top of COLLINS, who's on the table. THEY kiss.)

ANGEL, COLLINS, MAUREEN, MARK, and MR. GREY
BROTHERS!

MARK, ANGEL, MIMI, and THREE OTHERS
BISEXUALS, TRISEXUALS, HOMO SAPIENS
CARCINOGENS, HALLUCINOGENS, MEN, PEE-WEE HERMAN
GERMAN WINE, TURPENTINE, GERTRUDE STEIN
ANTONIONI, BERTOLUCCI, KUROSAWA
"CARMINA BURANA"

ALL
TO APATHY, TO ENTROPY, TO EMPATHY, ECSTASY
VACLAV HAVEL—THE SEX PISTOLS, 8BC
TO NO SHAME—NEVER PLAYING THE FAME GAME

COLLINS
TO MARIJUANA

ALL
TO SODOMY
IT'S BETWEEN GOD AND ME
TO S & M

(MR. GREY walks out.)

BENNY
WAITER . . . WAITER . . . WAITER

ALL
LA VIE BOHÈME

COLLINS
IN HONOR OF THE DEATH OF BOHEMIA, AN IMPROMPTU SALON
WILL COMMENCE IMMEDIATELY FOLLOWING DINNER . . . MIMI
MARQUEZ, CLAD ONLY IN BUBBLE WRAP, WILL PERFORM HER
FAMOUS LAWN-CHAIR-HANDCUFF DANCE TO THE SOUNDS OF
ICE TEA BEING STIRRED

ROGER
MARK COHEN WILL PREVIEW HIS NEW DOCUMENTARY ABOUT
HIS INABILITY TO HOLD AN ERECTION ON THE HIGH HOLY DAYS

(ROGER picks up an electric guitar and starts to tune it.)

MARK
AND MAUREEN JOHNSON, BACK FROM HER SPECTACULAR
ONE-NIGHT ENGAGEMENT AT THE 11TH STREET LOT, WILL SING
NATIVE AMERICAN TRIBAL CHANTS BACKWARD THROUGH HER
VOCODER, WHILE ACCOMPANYING HERSELF ON THE ELECTRIC
CELLO— WHICH SHE HAS NEVER STUDIED

(By this point, JOANNE has entered and seen MAUREEN playfully kiss MARK. JOANNE exits. BENNY pulls MIMI aside.)

BENNY
YOUR NEW BOYFRIEND DOESN'T KNOW ABOUT US?

MIMI
THERE'S NOTHING TO KNOW

BENNY
DON'T YOU THINK THAT WE COULD DISCUSS—

MIMI
IT WAS THREE MONTHS AGO

BENNY
HE DOESN'T ACT LIKE HE'S WITH YOU

MIMI
WE'RE TAKING IT SLOW

BENNY
WHERE IS HE NOW?

MIMI
HE'S RIGHT—HMM

BENNY
UH-HUH

MIMI
WHERE'D HE GO?

MARK
ROGER WILL ATTEMPT TO WRITE A BITTERSWEET, PROVOCATIVE SONG.

(ROGER starts to play Musetta's theme.)

THAT DOESN'T REMIND US OF "MUSETTA'S WALTZ"

COLLINS

ANGEL DUMOTT SCHUNARD WILL MODEL THE LATEST FALL
FASHIONS FROM PARIS WHILE ACCOMPANYING HERSELF ON
THE TEN-GALLON PLASTIC PICKLE-TUB.

ANGEL

AND COLLINS WILL RECOUNT HIS EXPLOITS AS AN ANARCHIST—
INCLUDING THE TALE OF HIS SUCCESSFUL REPROGRAMMING OF
THE MIT VIRTUAL-REALITY EQUIPMENT TO SELF-DESTRUCT, AS IT
BROADCASTS THE WORDS

ALL

"ACTUAL REALITY—ACT UP—FIGHT AIDS"

BENNY

CHECK!!

(BENNY exits. Lights on MIMI and ROGER.)

MIMI

EXCUSE ME—DID I DO SOMETHING WRONG?
I GET INVITED—THEN IGNORED—ALL NIGHT LONG

ROGER

I'VE BEEN TRYING—I'M NOT LYING
NO ONE'S PERFECT—I'VE GOT BAGGAGE

MIMI

LIFE'S TOO SHORT—BABE—TIME IS FLYING
I'M LOOKING FOR BAGGAGE THAT GOES WITH MINE

ROGER

I SHOULD TELL YOU—

MIMI

I'VE GOT BAGGAGE TOO

ROGER

I SHOULD TELL YOU—

BOTH

BAGGAGE—WINE—

OTHERS

AND BEER!

(Several beepers go off. Each person turns his or her own off.)

MIMI

AZT BREAK

(MIMI, ROGER, ANGEL, and COLLINS take pills.)

ROGER

YOU?

MIMI

ME. YOU?

ROGER

MIMI.

(They hold hands and stare into each other's eyes lovingly. The rest of the COMPANY freezes.)

24. I Should Tell You

ROGER

I SHOULD TELL YOU I'M DISASTER
I FORGET HOW TO BEGIN IT

MIMI

LET'S JUST MAKE THIS PART GO FASTER
I HAVE YET—TO BE IN IT
I SHOULD TELL YOU

ROGER

I SHOULD TELL YOU

MIMI

I SHOULD TELL YOU

ROGER

I SHOULD TELL YOU

MIMI

I SHOULD TELL YOU I BLEW THE CANDLE OUT
JUST TO GET BACK IN

ROGER

I'D FORGOTTEN HOW TO SMILE
UNTIL YOUR CANDLE BURNED MY SKIN

MIMI

I SHOULD TELL YOU

ROGER

I SHOULD TELL YOU

MIMI

I SHOULD TELL YOU

BOTH

I SHOULD TELL
WELL, HERE WE GO
NOW WE—

MIMI

OH NO

ROGER

I KNOW—THIS SOMETHING IS
HERE GOES—

MIMI

HERE GOES

ROGER

GUESS SO
IT'S STARTING TO
WHO KNOWS—

MIMI

WHO KNOWS

BOTH

WHO KNOWS WHERE
WHO GOES THERE
WHO KNOWS
HERE GOES

TRUSTING DESIRE—STARTING TO LEARN
WALKING THROUGH FIRE WITHOUT A BURN
CLINGING—A SHOULDER, A LEAP BEGINS
STINGING AND OLDER, ASLEEP ON PINS

SO HERE WE GO
NOW WE—

ROGER

OH NO

MIMI

I KNOW

ROGER

OH NO

BOTH

WHO KNOWS WHERE—WHO GOES THERE
HERE GOES—HERE GOES
HERE GOES—HERE GOES
HERE GOES—HERE GOES

Jonathan Larson

Anthony Rapp as Mark Cohen

Daphne Rubin-Vega as Mimi Marquez

Anthony Rapp as Mark Cohen, left,
and Adam Pascal as Roger Davis

Jesse L. Martin as Tom Collins, left, and
Wilson Jermaine Heredia as Angel Schunard

Adam Pascal as Roger Davis, left,
and Anthony Rapp as Mark Cohen

Anthony Rapp as Mark Cohen, left,
and Jesse L. Martin as Tom Collins

Left to right: Jesse L. Martin as Tom Collins, Anthony Rapp
as Mark Cohen, and Taye Diggs as Benjamin Coffin III

Fredi Walker as Joanne Jefferson, left,
and Idina Menzel as Maureen Johnson

Jesse L. Martin as Tom Collins, top left, and the Company

Adam Pascal as Roger Davis and
Daphne Rubin-Vega as Mimi Marquez

Left to right: Adam Pascal as Roger Davis, Daphne Rubin-Vega
as Mimi Marquez, and Anthony Rapp as Mark Cohen

Left to right: Anthony Rapp as Mark Cohen, Adam Pascal as
Roger Davis, Daphne Rubin-Vega as Mimi Marquez, Idina Menzel
as Maureen Johnson, and Fredi Walker as Joanne Jefferson

Bottom left to right: Fredi Walker as Joanne Jefferson, Daphne
Rubin-Vega as Mimi Marquez, Adam Pascal as Roger Davis, Taye
Diggs as Benjamin Coffin III, Jesse L. Martin as Tom Collins, and
Wilson Jermaine Heredia as Angel Schunard

The Company

The Company

25. La Vie Bohème B

(ROGER and MIMI exit. JOANNE reenters, obviously steamed.)

                    MAUREEN
ARE WE PACKED?

                    JOANNE
YES AND BY NEXT WEEK
I WANT YOU TO BE

                    MAUREEN
POOKIE?

                    JOANNE
AND YOU SHOULD SEE
THEY'VE PADLOCKED YOUR BUILDING
AND THEY'RE RIOTING ON AVENUE B
BENNY CALLED THE COPS

                    MAUREEN
THAT FUCK

                    JOANNE
THEY DON'T KNOW WHAT THEY'RE DOING
THE COPS ARE SWEEPING THE LOT
BUT NO ONE'S LEAVING
THEY'RE SITTING THERE, MOOING!

                    ALL
YEA!!!

(Pandemonium erupts in the restaurant.)

                    ALL
TO DANCE!

A GIRL
NO WAY TO MAKE A LIVING, MASOCHISM, PAIN, PERFECTION
MUSCLE SPASMS, CHIROPRACTORS, SHORT-CAREERS, EATING
DISORDERS

ALL
FILM

MARK
ADVENTURE, TEDIUM, NO FAMILY, BORING LOCATIONS
DARKROOMS, PERFECT FACES, EGOS, MONEY, HOLLYWOOD
AND SLEAZE

ALL
MUSIC

ANGEL
FOOD OF LOVE, EMOTION, MATHEMATICS, ISOLATION, RHYTHM
POWER, FEELING, HARMONY AND HEAVY COMPETITION

ALL
ANARCHY

COLLINS and MAUREEN
REVOLUTION, JUSTICE, SCREAMING FOR SOLUTIONS
FORCING CHANGES, RISK AND DANGER, MAKING NOISE AND
MAKING PLEAS

ALL
TO FAGGOTS, LEZZIES, DYKES, CROSS DRESSERS TOO

MAUREEN
TO ME

MARK
TO ME

COLLINS and ANGEL
TO ME

ALL

TO YOU, AND YOU AND YOU, YOU AND YOU
TO PEOPLE LIVING WITH, LIVING WITH, LIVING WITH
NOT DYING FROM DISEASE
LET HE AMONG US WITHOUT SIN
BE THE FIRST TO CONDEMN
LA VIE BOHÈME
LA VIE BOHÈME
LA VIE BOHÈME

MARK	**ALL**
ANYONE OUT OF THE MAINSTREAM?	LA VIE BOHÈME
IS ANYONE IN THE MAINSTREAM?	
ANYONE ALIVE—WITH A SEX DRIVE	LA VIE BOHÈME
TEAR DOWN THE WALL	
AREN'T WE ALL	LA VIE BOHÈME
THE OPPOSITE OF WAR ISN'T PEACE . . .	
IT'S CREATION	

ALL

LA VIE BOHÈME

MARK

The riot continues. The Christmas tree goes up in flames. The snow dances. Oblivious, Mimi and Roger share a small, lovely kiss.

ALL

Viva la Vie Bohème

Act Two

(The COMPANY enters from all directions and forms a line across the apron of the stage.)

26. Seasons of Love

COMPANY
FIVE HUNDRED TWENTY-FIVE THOUSAND
SIX HUNDRED MINUTES
FIVE HUNDRED TWENTY-FIVE THOUSAND
MOMENTS SO DEAR
FIVE HUNDRED TWENTY-FIVE THOUSAND
SIX HUNDRED MINUTES
HOW DO YOU MEASURE—MEASURE A YEAR?

IN DAYLIGHTS—IN SUNSETS
IN MIDNIGHTS—IN CUPS OF COFFEE
IN INCHES—IN MILES
IN LAUGHTER—IN STRIFE

IN—FIVE HUNDRED TWENTY-FIVE THOUSAND
SIX HUNDRED MINUTES
HOW DO YOU MEASURE
A YEAR IN THE LIFE?

HOW ABOUT LOVE?
HOW ABOUT LOVE?
HOW ABOUT LOVE?
HOW ABOUT LOVE?
SEASONS OF LOVE
SEASONS OF LOVE

SOLOIST #1
FIVE HUNDRED TWENTY-FIVE THOUSAND
SIX HUNDRED MINUTES
FIVE HUNDRED TWENTY-FIVE THOUSAND
JOURNEYS TO PLAN

FIVE HUNDRED TWENTY-FIVE THOUSAND
SIX HUNDRED MINUTES
HOW DO YOU MEASURE THE LIFE
OF A WOMAN OR A MAN?

SOLOIST #2
IN TRUTHS THAT SHE LEARNED
OR IN TIMES THAT HE CRIED
IN BRIDGES HE BURNED
OR THE WAY THAT SHE DIED

ALL
IT'S TIME NOW—TO SING OUT
THO' THE STORY NEVER ENDS
LET'S CELEBRATE
REMEMBER A YEAR IN THE LIFE OF FRIENDS

REMEMBER THE LOVE
REMEMBER THE LOVE
REMEMBER THE LOVE
MEASURE IN LOVE

SOLOIST #1
MEASURE, MEASURE YOU LIFE IN LOVE SEASONS OF LOVE
SEASONS OF LOVE

27. Happy New Year

The street

(New Year's Eve. The street outside the apartment. One table is on its end and serves as the "door.")

MARK
(carrying mock door)
Pan to the padlocked door. New Year's-Rocking Eve. The breaking-back-into-the-building party . . .

(ROGER and MIMI try in vain to pry a padlock from the door. They're happy.)

MIMI

HOW LONG 'TIL NEXT YEAR?

ROGER

THREE AND A HALF MINUTES . . .

MIMI

I'M GIVING UP MY VICES
I'M GOING BACK—BACK TO SCHOOL
EVICTION OR NOT
THIS WEEK'S BEEN SO HOT
THAT LONG AS I'VE GOT YOU
I KNOW I'LL BE COOL

I COULDN'T CRACK THE LOVE CODE, DEAR
'TIL YOU MADE THE LOCK ON MY HEART EXPLODE
IT'S GONNA BE A HAPPY NEW YEAR
A HAPPY NEW YEAR

(MARK enters the scene.)

MARK

COAST IS CLEAR
YOU'RE SUPPOSED TO BE WORKING
THAT'S FOR MIDNIGHT
WHERE ARE THEY?
THERE ISN'T MUCH TIME

MIMI

MAYBE THEY'RE DRESSING
I MEAN, WHAT DOES ONE WEAR THAT'S APROPOS
FOR A PARTY—THAT'S ALSO A CRIME

(MAUREEN enters wearing a skin tight "cat burglar" suit, holding a bag of potato chips.)

MAUREEN

CHIPS, ANYONE?

MARK

YOU CAN TAKE THE GIRL OUT OF HICKSVILLE
BUT YOU CAN'T TAKE THE HICKSVILLE OUT OF THE GIRL

MAUREEN

MY RIOT GOT YOU ON TV
I DESERVE A ROYALTY

MIMI

BE NICE, YOU TWO
OR NO GOD-AWFUL CHAMPAGNE

(MAUREEN takes out a cellular phone and dials.)

MAUREEN

DON'T MIND IF I DO
NO LUCK?

ROGER

BOLTED PLYWOOD, PADLOCKED WITH A CHAIN
A TOTAL DEAD END

MAUREEN

JUST LIKE ME EX-GIRLFRIEND
                    (on cellular phone)
HONEY . . . ?
I KNOW YOU'RE THERE . . .
PLEASE PICK UP THE PHONE
ARE YOU OKAY?
IT'S NOT FUNNY
IT'S NOT FAIR
HOW CAN I ATONE?
ARE YOU OKAY?
I LOSE CONTROL
BUT I CAN LEARN TO BEHAVE
GIVE ME ONE MORE CHANCE
LET ME BE YOUR SLAVE

I'LL KISS YOUR DOC MARTENS
LET ME KISS YOUR DOC MARTENS
YOUR EVERY WISH I WILL OBEY

(JOANNE enters.)

                    JOANNE

THAT MIGHT BE OKAY
DOWN GIRL
HEEL . . . STAY

I DID A BIT RESEARCH
WITH MY FRIENDS AT LEGAL AID
TECHNICALLY, YOU'RE SQUATTERS
THERE'S HOPE
BUT JUST IN CASE

(JOANNE whips out . . .)

                MARK and JOANNE
ROPE!

                    MARK
                (pointing off)
WE CAN HOIST A LINE—

                    JOANNE
TO THE FIRE ESCAPE—

                    MARK
AND TIE OFF AT

                MARK and JOANNE
THAT BENCH!

                    MAUREEN
I CAN'T TAKE THEM AS CHUMS

JOANNE
START HOISTING . . . WENCH

(ALL THREE cross upstage and attempt to throw the rope over a plank above. ROGER and MIMI laugh in each others arms.)

ROGER
I THINK I SHOULD BE LAUGHING
YET I FORGET
FORGET HOW TO BEGIN

I'M FEELING SOMETHING INSIDE
AND YET I STILL CAN'T DECIDE
IF I SHOULD HIDE
OR MAKE A WIDE-OPEN GRIN

LAST WEEK I WANTED JUST TO DISAPPEAR
MY LIFE WAS DUST
BUT NOW IT JUST MAY BE A HAPPY NEW YEAR
A HAPPY NEW YEAR

(COLLINS and ANGEL enter. COLLINS, in full black, carries a bottle of champagne. ANGEL is in a blond wig and plastic dress, with a small blowtorch slung around his shoulder.)

COLLINS
BOND—JAMES BOND

ANGEL
AND PUSSY GALORE—IN PERSON

MIMI
PUSSY—YOU CAME PREPARED

ANGEL
I WAS A BOY SCOUT ONCE
AND A BROWNIE
'TIL SOME BRAT GOT SCARED

COLLINS
(to MIMI)
AHA! MONEYPENNY—MY MARTINI!

MIMI
WILL BAD CHAMPAGNE DO?

ROGER
THAT'S SHAKEN—NOT STIRRED

COLLINS
PUSSY—THE BOLTS

(COLLINS takes a swig of champagne as ANGEL retrieves the small blowtorch.)

ANGEL
JUST SAY THE WORD!

(ANGEL turns on the torch. Lights to black.)

MIMI
TWO MINUTES LEFT TO EXECUTE OUR PLAN

COLLINS
WHERE'S EVERYONE ELSE?

ROGER
PLAYING SPIDER-MAN

MARK
IRONIC CLOSE UP: TIGHT

ON THE PHONE MACHINE'S RED LIGHT
ONCE THE BOHO BOYS ARE GONE
THE POWER MYSTERIOUSLY COMES ON

28. Voice Mail #3

(Light up on MRS. COHEN, who's standing on a chair and holding up a phone.)

MRS. COHEN
MARK, IT'S THE WICKED WITCH OF THE WEST
YOUR MOTHER
HAPPY NEW YEAR FROM SCARSDALE
WE'RE ALL IMPRESSED THAT THE RIOT FOOTAGE
MADE THE NIGHTLY NEWS
EVEN YOUR FATHER SAYS MAZEL TOV
HONEY—CALL HIM.
LOVE, MOM

(MRS. COHEN, stepping off the chair, passes the phone to ALEXI DARLING.)

ALEXI DARLING
(on chair)
MARK COHEN
ALEXI DARLING FROM *BUZZLINE*

MARK
Oh, that show's so sleazy.

ALEXI DARLING
YOUR FOOTAGE ON THE RIOTS A-ONE
FEATURE-SEGMENT-NETWORK-DEAL TIME
I'M SENDING YOU A CONTRACT
KER-CHING, KER-CHING
MARKY, GIVE US A CALL
970-4301
OR AT HOME TRY 863-6754
OR—MY CELL PHONE AT 919-763-0090
OR—YOU CAN E-MAIL ME
AT DARLING ALEXI NEWSCOM DOT NET
OR—YOU CAN PAGE ME AT—
(Beeeep!)

29. Happy New Year B

MAUREEN
I THINK WE NEED AN AGENT

MARK
WE?

JOANNE
THAT'S SELLING OUT

MARK
BUT IT'S NICE TO DREAM

MAUREEN
YEAH—IT'S NETWORK TV
AND IT'S ALL THANKS TO ME

MARK
SOMEHOW I THINK I SMELL
THE WHIFF OF A SCHEME

JOANNE
ME TOO

MAUREEN
WE CAN PLAN ANOTHER PROTEST

JOANNE
WE?!

MAUREEN
THIS TIME YOU CAN SHOOT FROM THE START . . .
                    (to MARK)
YOU'LL DIRECT
                    (to JOANNE)
STARRING ME!

(Lights shift back to downstairs.)

ALL
FIVE, FOUR, THREE . . . OPEN SESAME!!

(The door falls away, revealing MARK, JOANNE, and MAUREEN.)

HAPPY NEW YEAR
HAPPY NEW YEAR
HAPPY NEW . . .

(BENNY enters.)

BENNY
I SEE THAT YOU'VE BEATEN ME TO THE PUNCH

ROGER
HOW DID YOU KNOW WE'D BE HERE?

BENNY
I HAD A HUNCH

MARK
YOU'RE NOT MAD?

BENNY
I'M HERE TO END THIS WAR
IT'S A SHAME YOU WENT AND DESTROYED THE DOOR

MIMI
WHY ALL THE SUDDEN THE BIG ABOUT-FACE

BENNY
THE CREDIT IS YOURS
YOU MADE A GOOD CASE

ROGER
WHAT CASE?

BENNY
MIMI CAME TO SEE ME
AND SHE HAD MUCH TO SAY

MIMI
THAT'S NOT HOW YOU PUT IT AT ALL YESTERDAY

BENNY
I COULDN'T STOP THINKING ABOUT THE WHOLE MESS
MARK—YOU MIGHT WANT THIS ON FILM

(MARK picks up his camera.)

MARK
I GUESS

BENNY
(formally)
I REGRET THE
UNLUCKY CIRCUMSTANCES
OF THE PAST SEVEN DAYS

ROGER
CIRCUMSTANCE?
YOU PADLOCKED OUR DOOR

BENNY
AND IT'S WITH GREAT PLEASURE
ON BEHALF OF CYBERARTS
THAT I HAND YOU THIS KEY

(BENNY hands ROGER the key.)

ANGEL
GOLF CLAPS

(THEY oblige.)

MARK
I HAD NO JUICE IN MY BATTERY

BENNY
RESHOOT

ROGER
I SEE—THIS IS A PHOTO OPPORTUNITY

MAUREEN
THE BENEVOLENT GOD
USHERS THE POOR ARTISTS BACK TO THEIR FLAT
WERE YOU PLANNING TO TAKE DOWN THE BARBED WIRE
FROM THE LOT, TOO?

ROGER
ANYTHING BUT THAT!

BENNY
CLEARING THE LOT WAS A SAFETY CONCERN
WE BREAK GROUND THIS MONTH
BUT YOU CAN RETURN

MAUREEN
THAT'S WHY YOU'RE HERE WITH PEOPLE YOU HATE
INSTEAD OF WITH MUFFY AT MUFFY'S ESTATE

BENNY
I'D HONESTLY RATHER BE WITH YOU TONIGHT
THAN IN WESTPORT—

ROGER
SPARE US, OLD SPORT, THE SOUND BITE

BENNY
MIMI—SINCE YOUR WAYS ARE SO SEDUCTIVE

MIMI
YOU CAME ON TO ME!

BENNY
PERSUADE HIM NOT TO BE SO COUNTERPRODUCTIVE

ROGER
LIAR!

BENNY

WHY NOT TELL THEM WHAT YOU WORE TO MY PLACE?

MIMI

I WAS ON MY WAY TO WORK

BENNY

BLACK LEATHER AND LACE!
MY DESK WAS A MESS
I THINK I'M STILL SORE

MIMI

'CAUSE I KICKED HIM AND TOLD HIM I WASN'T HIS WHORE!

BENNY

DOES YOUR BOYFRIEND KNOW
WHO YOUR LAST BOYFRIEND WAS?

ROGER

I'M NOT HER BOYFRIEND
I DON'T CARE WHAT SHE DOES

ANGEL

PEOPLE! IS THIS ANY WAY TO START A NEW YEAR?
HAVE COMPASSION
BENNY JUST LOST HIS CAT

BENNY

MY DOG—BUT I APPRECIATE THAT

ANGEL

MY CAT HAD A FALL
AND I WENT THROUGH HELL

BENNY

IT'S LIKE LOSING A—
HOW DID YOU KNOW THAT SHE FELL?

COLLINS
(hands BENNY a glass of champagne)
CHAMPAGNE?

BENNY
DON'T MIND IF I DO
TO DOGS

ALL BUT BENNY
NO BENNY—TO YOU!

ANGEL
LET'S MAKE A RESOLUTION

MIMI
I'LL DRINK TO THAT

COLLINS
LET'S ALWAYS STAY FRIENDS

JOANNE
THO' WE MAY HAVE OUR DISPUTES

MAUREEN
THIS FAMILY TREE'S GOT DEEP ROOTS

MARK
FRIENDSHIP IS THICKER THAN BLOOD

ROGER
THAT DEPENDS

MIMI
DEPENDS ON TRUST

ROGER
DEPENDS ON TRUE DEVOTION

JOANNE
DEPENDS ON LOVE

MARK
(to ROGER)
DEPENDS ON NOT DENYING EMOTION

ROGER

PERHAPS

ALL
IT'S GONNA BE A HAPPY NEW YEAR

ROGER

I GUESS

ALL
IT'S GONNA BE A HAPPY NEW YEAR

ROGER

YOU'RE RIGHT

(ANGEL brings ROGER and MIMI together. ANGEL and OTHERS move away from MIMI and ROGER.)

ANGEL
IT'S GONNA BE A HAPPY NEW YEAR

ROGER and MIMI

I'M SORRY

ROGER

COMING?

MIMI
IN A MINUTE—I'M FINE—GO

(ROGER kisses MIMI and exits. THE MAN appears.)

THE MAN
WELL, WELL, WELL. WHAT HAVE WE HERE?

(THE MAN moves to MIMI and holds out a small plastic bag of
white powder.)

IT'S GONNA BE A HAPPY NEW YEAR
THERE, THERE . . . ETC.

(Fade out.)

30. Take Me or Leave Me

Any location and JOANNE's loft

MARK

Valentine's Day . . . pan across the empty lot. Roger's down at
Mimi's, where he's been for almost two months now, although he
keeps talking about selling his guitar and heading out of town. (Still
jealous of Benny) . . . God knows where Collins and Angel are. . . .
Could be that new shantytown near the river or a suite at the
Plaza. . . . Maureen and Joanne are rehearsing.

JOANNE

I said—once more from the top!

MAUREEN

I said no!!

MARK

That is if they're still speaking this week. . . . Me? I'm here. Nowhere.
(Lights up on the scene.)

JOANNE

And the line is, "Cyberarts and it's corporate sponsor, Grey
Communications, would like to mitigate the Christmas Eve riots . . ."
What is so difficult . . . ?

MAUREEN

It just doesn't roll off my tongue. I like my version.

JOANNE

You—dressed as a groundhog—to protest the groundbreaking . . .

MAUREEN

It's a metaphor!

JOANNE

It's . . . less than brilliant.

MAUREEN

That's it, Miss Ivy League!

JOANNE

What?

MAUREEN

Ever since New Year's, I haven't said boo. I let you direct. I didn't pierce my nipples because it grossed you out. I didn't stay and dance at the Clit Club that night 'cause you wanted to go home . . .

JOANNE

You were flirting with the woman in rubber.

MAUREEN

That's what this is about? There will always be women in rubber—flirting with me! Give me a break.

MAUREEN

EVERY SINGLE DAY
I WALK DOWN THE STREET
I HEAR PEOPLE SAY
"BABY'S SO SWEET"

EVER SINCE PUBERTY
EVERYBODY STARES AT ME
BOYS—GIRLS
I CAN'T HELP IT, BABY

SO BE KIND
DON'T LOSE YOUR MIND

JUST REMEMBER THAT I'M YOUR BABY

TAKE ME FOR WHAT I AM
WHO I WAS MEANT TO BE
AND IF YOU GIVE A DAMN T
AKE ME, BABY, OR LEAVE ME
TAKE ME, BABY, OR LEAVE ME

A TIGER IN A CAGE
CAN NEVER SEE THE SUN
THIS DIVA NEEDS HER STAGE
BABY—LET'S HAVE FUN!

YOU ARE THE ONE I CHOOSE
FOLKS'D KILL TO FILL YOUR SHOES
YOU LOVE THE LIMELIGHT TOO, BABY

SO BE MINE OR DON'T WASTE MY TIME
CRYIN'—"HONEYBEAR—ARE YOU STILL MY BABY?"

TAKE ME FOR WHAT I AM
WHO I WAS MEANT TO BE
AND IF YOU GIVE A DAMN
TAKE ME, BABY, OR LEAVE ME
NO WAY CAN I BE WHAT I'M NOT
BUT HEY—DON'T YOU WANT YOUR GIRL HOT!
DON'T FIGHT—DON'T LOSE YOUR HEAD

'CAUSE EVERY NIGHT—WHO'S IN YOUR BED?
WHO'S IN YOUR BED, BABY?

(MAUREEN pouts in JOANNE'S direction.)

Kiss, Pookie.

JOANNE
It won't work.
I LOOK BEFORE I LEAP
I LOVE MARGINS AND DISCIPLINE

I MAKE LISTS IN MY SLEEP
BABY, WHAT'S MY SIN?

NEVER QUIT—I FOLLOW THROUGH
I HATE MESS—BUT I LOVE YOU
WHAT TO DO
WITH MY IMPROMPTU BABY

SO BE WISE
THIS GIRL SATISFIES
YOU'VE GOT A PRIZE
WHO DON'T COMPROMISE
YOU'RE ONE LUCKY BABY
TAKE ME FOR WHAT I AM

                    MAUREEN

A CONTROL FREAK

                    JOANNE

WHO I WAS MEANT TO BE

                    MAUREEN

A SNOB—YET OVERATTENTIVE

                    JOANNE

AND IF YOU GIVE A DAMN

                    MAUREEN

A LOVABLE, DROLL GEEK

                    JOANNE

TAKE ME, BABY, OR LEAVE ME

                    MAUREEN

AND ANAL RETENTIVE!

                      BOTH

THAT'S IT!

JOANNE

THE STRAW THAT BREAKS MY BACK

BOTH

I QUIT

JOANNE

UNLESS YOU TAKE IT BACK

BOTH

WOMEN

MAUREEN

WHAT IS IT ABOUT THEM?

BOTH

CAN'T LIVE—
WITH THEM—OR WITHOUT THEM!
TAKE ME FOR WHAT I AM
WHO I WAS MEANT TO BE
AND IF YOU GIVE A DAMN
TAKE ME, BABY, OR LEAVE ME
TAKE ME, BABY
OR LEAVE ME
GUESS I'M LEAVIN'
I'M GONE!

(JOANNE and MAUREEN both sit.)

31. Seasons of Love B

COMPANY

IN DIAPERS—REPORT CARDS
IN SPOKED WHEELS—IN SPEEDING TICKETS
IN CONTRACTS—DOLLARS
IN FUNERALS—IN BIRTHS
IN—FIVE HUNDRED TWENTY-FIVE THOUSAND
SIX HUNDRED MINUTES

HOW DO YOU FIGURE
A LAST YEAR ON EARTH?

FIGURE IN LOVE
FIGURE IN LOVE
FIGURE IN LOVE
MEASURE IN LOVE
SEASONS OF LOVE
SEASONS OF LOVE

32. Without You

Mimi's Apartment

(Three beds appear downstage. One is a hospital bed, occupied by ANGEL. ROGER sits on one. JOANNE is on the other. MIMI approaches ROGER, and appears to be in a hurry.)

ROGER

Where were you?

MIMI

I'm sorry, I'm late . . .

ROGER
(interrupting)
I know. You lost your keys. No, you went for a walk; you had to help your mother.

ROGER
(as he picks up the guitar)
How's Benny? I'm gonna work upstairs tonight.

MIMI

WAIT . . .
I SHOULD TELL YOU
I SHOULD . . .
NEVER MIND . . .

ROGER

HAPPY SPRING

(ROGER exits. MIMI reveals a just purchased stash bag and angrily flings it across the room. As MIMI sings the following, a stylized "musical bed" is choreographed around her. During the bridge of the song, ANGEL is carried from the hospital bed by COLLINS and is replaced by ROGER. By the end of the song, JOANNE and MAUREEN are reunited as are ROGER and MIMI. COLLINS and ANGEL have laid down together, where ANGEL dies.)

MIMI

WITHOUT YOU
THE GROUND THAWS
THE RAIN FALLS
THE GRASS GROWS

WITHOUT YOU
THE SEEDS ROOT
THE FLOWERS BLOOM
THE CHILDREN PLAY

THE STARS GLEAM
THE POETS DREAM
THE EAGLES FLY
WITHOUT YOU

THE EARTH TURNS
THE SUN BURNS
BUT I DIE
WITHOUT YOU

WITHOUT YOU
THE BREEZE WARMS
THE GIRL SMILES
THE CLOUD MOVES

WITHOUT YOU
THE TIDES CHANGE

THE BOYS RUN
THE OCEANS CRASH

THE CROWDS ROAR
THE DAYS SOAR
THE BABIES CRY
WITHOUT YOU

THE MOON GLOWS
THE RIVER FLOWS
BUT I DIE
WITHOUT YOU

ROGER

THE WORLD REVIVES

MIMI

COLORS RENEW

BOTH

BUT I KNOW BLUE
ONLY BLUE
LONELY BLUE
WITHIN ME, BLUE
WITHOUT YOU

MIMI

WITHOUT YOU
THE HAND GROPES
THE EAR HEARS
THE PULSE BEATS

ROGER

WITHOUT YOU
THE EYES GAZE
THE LEGS WALK
THE LUNGS BREATH

                        BOTH
THE MIND CHURNS
THE HEART YEARNS
THE TEARS DRY
WITHOUT YOU

LIFE GOES ON
BUT I'M GONE
'CAUSE I DIE

                        ROGER
WITHOUT YOU

                        MIMI
WITHOUT YOU

                        ROGER
WITHOUT YOU

                        BOTH
WITHOUT YOU

33. Voice Mail #4

The loft

(The phone rings . . .)

        ROGER and MARK'S ANSWERING MACHINE
SPEAK . . .
  (BEEEP!)

                ALEXI DARLING
MARK COHEN
ALEXI DARLING
LABOR DAY WEEKEND
IN EAST HAMPTON

ON THE BEACH
JUST SAW ALEC BALDWIN
TOLD HIM YOU SAY HI
JUST KIDDING

WE STILL NEED DIRECTORS
YOU STILL NEED MONEY
YOU KNOW YOU NEED MONEY
PICK UP THE PHONE
DON'T BE AFRAID OF KER-CHING, KER-CHING

MARKY—SELL US YOUR SOUL
JUST KIDDING
WE'RE WAITING . . .

34. Contact

Various fantasy bed locales

(There are two main groups. As the music begins, a group of dancers
start a sensual life-and-death dance, while a group of actors gather
around a table centerstage to speaks words of passion, which
punctuates the dancing. Eventually the actors converge on the table
and cover themselves with a white sheet. ANGEL emerges upstage
of the sheeted group.)

GROUP A (ROGER, MARK, JOANNE, and BENNY)
HOT-HOT-HOT-SWEAT-SWEET
WET-WET-WET-RED-HEAT
HOT-HOT-HOT-SWEAT-SWEET
WET-WET-WET-RED-HEAT

PLEASE DON'T STOP PLEASE
PLEASE DON'T STOP STOP
STOP STOP STOP DON'T
PLEASE PLEASE PLEASE PLEASE
HOT-HOT-HOT-SWEAT-SWEET
WET-WET-WET-RED-HEAT

STICKY-LICKY-TRICKLE-TICKLE
STEAMY-CREAMY-STROKING-SOAKING

GROUP B (MIMI, COLLINS, MAUREEN, and ANGEL)
HOT-HOT-HOT-SWEAT-SWEET-WET-WET-WET-RED-HEAT

               COLLINS
TOUCH!

               MAUREEN
TASTE!

               MIMI
DEEP!

               COLLINS
DARK!

               MAUREEN
KISS!

               COLLINS
BEG!

               MIMI
SLAP!

      MIMI, MAUREEN, and COLLINS
FEAR!

               COLLINS
THICK!

      COLLINS, MIMI, and MAUREEN
RED, RED RED, RED
RED, RED—PLEASE

               MAUREEN
HARDER

ANGEL

FASTER

MAUREEN

WETTER

MIMI

BASTARD

COLLINS

YOU WHORE

MAUREEN

YOU CANNIBAL

MIMI and ANGEL

MORE

MAUREEN

YOU ANIMAL

MAUREEN, COLLINS, and MIMI

FLUID NO FLUID NO CONTACT YES NO CONTACT

ALL

FIRE FIRE BURN—BURN YES!
NO LATEX RUBBER RUBBER
FIRE LATEX RUBBER LATEX BUMMER LOVER BUMMER

(The music explodes into a fevered rhythmic heat as ANGEL is revealed in a lone spotlight, dancing wildly.)

ANGEL

TAKE ME
TAKE ME
TODAY FOR YOU
TOMORROW FOR ME
TODAY ME
TOMORROW YOU

TOMORROW YOU
LOVE
YOU
LOVE YOU
I LOVE YOU
I LOVE YOU I LOVE
YOU!
TAKE ME
TAKE ME
I LOVE YOU

(The music dies as ANGEL vanishes.)

                    ROGER'S VOICE
UM

                    JOANNE'S VOICE
WAIT

                    MIMI'S VOICE
SLIPPED

                    COLLINS' VOICE
SHIT

                    JOANNE'S VOICE
OW!

                    ROGER'S VOICE
WHERE'D IT GO?

                    MIMI'S VOICE
SAFE

                    COLLINS' VOICE
DAMN

                    MAUREEN'S VOICE
I THINK I MISSED—DON'T GET PISSED

ALL

IT WAS BAD FOR ME—WAS IT BAD FOR YOU?

JOANNE

IT'S OVER

MAUREEN

IT'S OVER

ROGER

IT'S OVER

MIMI

IT'S OVER

COLLINS

IT'S OVER

35. I'll Cover You: Reprise

In a church, ANGEL's memorial

MIMI

Angel was one of my closest friends. It's right that it's Halloween, because it was her favorite holiday. I knew we'd hit it off the moment we met—that skinhead was bothering her and she said she was more of a man than he'd ever be and more of a woman than he'd ever get . . .

MARK

. . . and then there was the time he walked up to this group of tourists—and they were petrified because (a)—they were obviously lost, and (b)—had probably never spoken to a drag queen before in their lives . . . and he . . . *she* just offered to escort them out of Alphabet City. . . . And then she let them take a picture with her— and then she said she'd help 'em find the Circle Line . . .

MAUREEN

. . . so much more original than any of us—you'd find an old tablecloth on the street and make a dress—and next year, sure enough—they'd be mass-producing them at the Gap! You always said how lucky you were that we were all friends—but it was us, baby, who were the lucky ones.

COLLINS

LIVE IN MY HOUSE
I'LL BE YOUR SHELTER
JUST PAY ME BACK WITH ONE THOUSAND KISSES
BE MY LOVER
AND I'LL COVER YOU

OPEN YOUR DOOR—
I'LL BE YOUR TENANT
DON'T GOT MUCH BAGGAGE
TO LAY AT YOUR FEET
BUT SWEET KISSES I'VE GOT TO SPARE
I'LL BE THERE—I'LL COVER YOU

I THINK THEY MEANT IT
WHEN THEY SAID YOU CAN'T BUY LOVE
NOW I KNOW YOU CAN RENT IT
A NEW LEASE YOU WERE, MY LOVE, ON LIFE

ALL MY LIFE
I'VE LONGED TO DISCOVER
SOMETHING AS TRUE
AS THIS IS

(The following is sung simultaneously.)

JOANNE and SOLOIST	COLLINS
SO WITH A THOUSAND SWEET KISSES I'LL COVER YOU	IF YOU'RE COLD AND YOU'RE LONELY
WITH A THOUSAND SWEET KISSES I'LL COVER YOU	YOU'VE GOT ONE NICKEL ONLY

WITH A THOUSAND SWEET KISSES
I'LL COVER YOU

WHEN YOU'RE WORN
OUT AND TIRED

WITH A THOUSAND SWEET KISSES
I'LL COVER YOU

WHEN YOUR HEART
HAS EXPIRED

COMPANY

FIVE HUNDRED TWENTY-FIVE THOUSAND SIX HUNDRED
MINUTES FIVE HUNDRED TWENTY-FIVE THOUSAND MOMENTS
SO DEAR
FIVE HUNDRED TWENTY-FIVE THOUSAND SIX HUNDRED
MINUTES
FIVE HUNDRED TWENTY-FIVE THOUSAND SIX HUNDRED—
MEASURE A YEAR
OH LOVER, I'LL COVER YOU
OH LOVER, I'LL COVER YOU

COLLINS and COMPANY

OH LOVER
I'LL COVER YOU
OH LOVER

COLLINS

OH LOVER
I'LL COVER YOU
OH LOVER

COLLINS

I'LL COVER YOU

COMPANY

FIVE HUNDRED TWENTY-FIVE THOUSAND SIX HUNDRED
MINUTES FIVE HUNDRED TWENTY-FIVE THOUSAND
SEASONS OF LOVE

COLLINS

I'LL COVER YOU

36. Halloween

Outside the Church

(MARK is on the pay phone.)

MARK

Hi. It's Mark Cohen. Is Alexi there? . . . No, don't bother her.
Just tell her I'm running a little late for our appointment. . . . Yes, I'm
still coming . . . Yes, I signed the contract . . . Thanks . . .

HOW DID WE GET HERE?
HOW THE HELL . . .
PAN LEFT—CLOSE ON THE STEEPLE OF THE CHURCH

HOW DID I GET HERE?
HOW THE HELL . . .
CHRISTMAS

CHRISTMAS EVE—LAST YEAR
HOW COULD A NIGHT SO FROZEN
BE SO SCALDING HOT?
HOW CAN A MORNING THIS MILD
BE SO RAW?

WHY ARE ENTIRE YEARS STREWN
ON THE CUTTING-ROOM FLOOR OF MEMORY
WHEN SINGLE FRAMES FROM ONE MAGIC NIGHT
FOREVER FLICKER IN CLOSE-UP
ON THE 3-D IMAX OF MY MIND

THAT'S POETIC
THAT'S PATHETIC

WHY DID MIMI KNOCK ON ROGER'S DOOR
AND COLLINS CHOOSE THAT PHONE BOOTH
BACK WHERE ANGEL SET UP HIS DRUMS?
WHY DID MAUREEN'S EQUIPMENT BREAK DOWN?

WHY AM I THE WITNESS?
AND WHEN I CAPTURE IT ON FILM
WILL IT MEAN THAT IT'S THE END
AND I'M ALONE

37. Goodbye, Love

(The principals emerge from the church.)

MIMI
(to ROGER)
IT'S TRUE YOU SOLD YOUR GUITAR AND BOUGHT A CAR?

ROGER
IT'S TRUE—I'M LEAVING NOW FOR SANTA FE
IT'S TRUE YOU'RE WITH THIS YUPPIE SCUM?

BENNY
YOU SAID—YOU'D NEVER SPEAK TO HIM AGAIN

MIMI
NOT NOW

MAUREEN
WHO SAID THAT YOU HAVE ANY SAY
IN WHO SHE SAYS THINGS TO AT ALL?

ROGER
YEAH!

JOANNE
WHO SAID THAT YOU SHOULD STICK YOUR NOSE IN
OTHER PEOPLE'S ...

MAUREEN
WHO SAID I WAS TALKING TO YOU?

JOANNE
WE USED TO HAVE THIS FIGHT
EACH NIGHT
SHE'D NEVER ADMIT
I EXISTED

MARK
CALM DOWN
EVERYONE, PLEASE

MIMI
HE WAS THE SAME WAY—HE WAS
ALWAYS
"RUN AWAY—HIT THE ROAD
DON'T COMMIT"—YOU'RE FULL
OF SHIT

BENNY
MIMI

JOANNE
SHE'S IN DENIAL

MIMI
HE'S IN DENIAL

JOANNE
DIDN'T GIVE AN INCH
WHEN I GAVE A MILE

MARK
COME ON

MIMI
I GAVE A MILE

ROGER
GAVE A MILE TO WHO?

MARK and BENNY
COME ON, GUYS, CHILL!

MIMI and JOANNE
I'D BE HAPPY TO DIE FOR A TASTE
OF WHAT ANGEL HAD
SOMEONE TO LIVE FOR—UNAFRAID
TO SAY I LOVE YOU

ROGER
ALL YOUR WORDS ARE NICE, MIMI
BUT LOVE'S NOT A THREE WAY STREET

YOU'LL NEVER SHARE REAL LOVE
UNTIL YOU LOVE YOUR SELF—I SHOULD KNOW

COLLINS
YOU ALL SAID YOU'D BE COOL TODAY
SO PLEASE—FOR MY SAKE . . .
I CAN'T BELIEVE HE'S GONE
(to ROGER)
I CAN'T BELIEVE YOU'RE GOING
I CAN'T BELIEVE THIS FAMILY MUST DIE
ANGEL HELPED US BELIEVE IN LOVE
I CAN'T BELIEVE YOU DISAGREE

ALL
I CAN'T BELIEVE THIS IS GOODBYE

(MAUREEN and JOANNE immediately burst into tears and embrace in front of all. COLLINS returns to the church. MIMI and BENNY leave together. ROGER and MARK are left alone.)

MAUREEN
POOKIE

JOANNE
HONEYBEAR

MAUREEN
I MISSED YOU SO MUCH

JOANNE
I MISSED YOU

MAUREEN
I MISSED YOUR SMELL

JOANNE
YOUR MOUTH
YOUR—

(JOANNE kisses MAUREEN firmly.)

MAUREEN

OW

JOANNE

WHAT?

MAUREEN

NOTHING, POOKIE

JOANNE

NO, BABY—YOU SAID "OW"—WHAT?

MAUREEN

YOU BIT MY TONGUE

JOANNE

NO, I DIDN'T

MAUREEN

YOU DID— I'M BLEEDING

JOANNE

NO, IT ISN'T

MAUREEN

I THINK I SHOULD KNOW . . .

JOANNE

LET ME SEE—

MAUREEN

SHE DOESN'T BELIEVE ME

JOANNE

I WAS ONLY TRYING TO . . .

(JOANNE and MAUREEN hug and exit. The PASTOR from the church emerges on the above.)

PASTOR

THOMAS B. COLLINS?

COLLINS

COMING

(The PASTOR exits above, and COLLINS exits into the church.
BENNY stands off to the side as MIMI approaches ROGER, who
turns away. MIMI hesitates before leaving with BENNY.)

MARK

I HEAR THERE ARE GREAT RESTAURANTS OUT WEST

ROGER

SOME OF THE BEST. HOW COULD SHE?

MARK

HOW COULD YOU LET HER GO?

ROGER

YOU JUST DON'T KNOW . . . HOW COULD WE LOSE ANGEL?

MARK

MAYBE YOU'LL SEE WHY WHEN YOU STOP ESCAPING YOUR PAIN
AT LEAST NOW IF YOU TRY—ANGEL'S DEATH WON'T BE IN VAIN

ROGER

HIS DEATH IS IN VAIN

(MIMI reappears up left, in the shadows. She overhears MARK and
ROGER's conversation.)

MARK

ARE YOU INSANE?
THERE'S SO MUCH TO CARE ABOUT
THERE'S ME—THERE'S MIMI—

ROGER

MIMI'S GOT HER BAGGAGE TOO

MARK

SO DO YOU

ROGER

WHO ARE YOU TO TELL ME WHAT I KNOW, WHAT TO DO

MARK

A FRIEND

ROGER

BUT WHO, MARK, ARE YOU?
"MARK HAS GOT HIS WORK"
THEY SAY
"MARK LIVES FOR HIS WORK"
AND "MARK'S IN LOVE WITH HIS WORK"
MARK HIDES IN HIS WORK

MARK

FROM WHAT?

ROGER

FACING YOUR FAILURE, FACING YOUR LONELINESS
FACING THE FACT YOU LIVE A LIE
YES, YOU LIVE A LIE—TELL YOU WHY

YOU'RE ALWAYS PREACHING NOT TO BE NUMB
WHEN THAT'S HOW YOU THRIVE
YOU PRETEND TO CREATE AND OBSERVE
WHEN YOU REALLY DETACH FROM FEELING ALIVE

MARK

PERHAPS'S IT'S BECAUSE I'M THE ONE OF US TO SURVIVE

ROGER

POOR BABY

MARK

MIMI STILL LOVES ROGER
IS ROGER REALLY JEALOUS
OR AFRAID THAT MIMI'S WEAK

ROGER

MIMI DID LOOK PALE

MARK

MIMI'S GOTTEN THIN
MIMI'S RUNNING OUT OF TIME
ROGER'S RUNNING OUT THE DOOR—

ROGER

NO MORE! OH NO!
I'VE GOTTA GO

MARK

HEY, FOR SOMEBODY WHO'S ALWAYS BEEN LET DOWN
WHO'S HEADING OUT OF TOWN?

ROGER

FOR SOMEONE WHO LONGS FOR A COMMUNITY OF HIS OWN
WHO'S WITH HIS CAMERA, ALONE?

(ROGER takes a step to go, then stops, turns.)

I'LL CALL
I HATE THE FALL

(ROGER turns to go and sees MIMI.)

YOU HEARD?

MIMI

EVERY WORD

YOU DON'T WANT BAGGAGE WITHOUT LIFETIME GUARANTEES
YOU DON'T WANT TO WATCH ME DIE?
I JUST CAME TO SAY
GOODBYE, LOVE
GOODBYE, LOVE
CAME TO SAY GOODBYE, LOVE, GOODBYE

MIMI	ROGER
JUST CAME TO SAY	GLORY
GOODBYE, LOVE	ONE BLAZE OF
GOODBYE, LOVE	GLORY
GOODBYE, LOVE	I HAVE TO FIND
GOODBYE	

(ROGER exits. BENNY returns. MIMI steps away.)

MIMI

PLEASE DON'T TOUCH ME
UNDERSTAND
I'M SCARED
I NEED TO GO AWAY

MARK

I KNOW A PLACE—A CLINIC

BENNY

A REHAB?

MIMI

MAYBE—COULD YOU?

BENNY

I'LL PAY

MIMI

GOODBYE, LOVE
GOODBYE, LOVE
CAME TO SAY GOODBYE, LOVE, GOODBYE

JUST CAME TO SAY
GOODBYE, LOVE
GOODBYE, LOVE
GOODBYE, LOVE

HELLO—DISEASE

(MIMI runs off. After a beat, COLLINS quickly enters, with the PASTOR behind him.)

38. What You Own

PASTOR
OFF THE PREMISES NOW
WE DON'T GIVE HANDOUTS HERE!

MARK
WHAT HAPPENED TO "REST IN PEACE"?

PASTOR
OFF THE PREMISES, QUEER!

(The PASTOR starts to exit.)

COLLINS
THAT'S NO WAY TO SEND A BOY
TO MEET HIS MAKER
THEY HAD TO KNOW
WE COULDN'T PAY THE UNDERTAKER

BENNY
DON'T WORRY 'BOUT HIM. HEY, I'LL TAKE CARE OF IT.

(The PASTOR acknowledges BENNY and exits.)

MARK
MUST BE NICE TO HAVE MONEY

ALL THREE
NO SHIT

COLLINS
I THINK IT'S ONLY FAIR TO TELL YOU
YOU JUST PAID FOR THE FUNERAL
OF THE PERSON WHO KILLED YOUR DOG

BENNY
I KNOW
I ALWAYS HATED THAT DOG
 LET'S PAY HIM OFF
AND THEN GET DRUNK

MARK
I CAN'T, I HAVE A MEETING

COLLINS and BENNY
PUNK! LET'S GO!

(COLLINS and BENNY exit.)

MARK
(imagining)
"Hi. Mark Cohen here for *Buzzline*. . . . Back to you, Alexi. Coming up next—Vampire welfare queens who are compulsive bowlers." Oh my God, what am I doing?

DON'T BREATHE TOO DEEP
DON'T THINK ALL DAY
DIVE INTO WORK
DRIVE THE OTHER WAY
THAT DRIP OF HURT
THAT PINT OF SHAME
GOES AWAY
JUST PLAY THE GAME

YOU'RE LIVING IN AMERICA
AT THE END OF THE MILLENNIUM
YOU'RE LIVING IN AMERICA
LEAVE YOUR CONSCIENCE AT THE TONE

AND WHEN YOU'RE LIVING IN AMERICA
AT THE END OF THE MILLENNIUM
YOU'RE WHAT YOU OWN

(Lights up on ROGER.)

ROGER
THE FILMMAKER CANNOT SEE

MARK
AND THE SONGWRITER CANNOT HEAR

ROGER
YET I SEE MIMI EVERYWHERE

MARK
ANGEL'S VOICE IS IN MY EAR

ROGER
JUST TIGHTEN THOSE SHOULDERS

MARK
JUST CLENCH YOUR JAW 'TIL YOU FROWN

ROGER
JUST DON'T LET GO

BOTH
OR YOU MAY DROWN

YOU'RE LIVING IN AMERICA
AT THE END OF THE MILLENNIUM
YOU'RE LIVING IN AMERICA
WHERE IT'S LIKE THE TWILIGHT ZONE

AND WHEN YOU'RE LIVING IN AMERICA
AT THE END OF THE MILLENNIUM
YOU'RE WHAT YOU OWN
SO I OWN NOT A NOTION
I ESCAPE AND APE CONTENT
I DON'T OWN EMOTION—I RENT

MARK	ROGER
WHAT WAS IT ABOUT THAT NIGHT	WHAT WAS IT ABOUT THAT NIGHT

BOTH
CONNECTION—IN AN ISOLATING AGE

MARK	ROGER
FOR ONCE THE SHADOWS GAVE WAY TO LIGHT	FOR ONCE THE SHADOWS GAVE WAY TO LIGHT

BOTH
FOR ONCE I DIDN'T DISENGAGE

(MARK goes to pay phone and dials.)

MARK
ANGEL—I HEAR YOU—I HEAR IT
I SEE IT—I SEE IT
MY FILM!

ROGER
MIMI—I SEE YOU—
I SEE IT
I HEAR IT—I HEAR IT
MY SONG!

MARK	ROGER
ALEXI- MARK	ONE SONG—GLORY
CALL ME A HYPOCRITE	MIMI
I NEED TO FINISH MY FILM	YOUR EYES
I QUIT!	

BOTH
DYING IN AMERICA
AT THE END OF THE MILLENNIUM
WE'RE DYING IN AMERICA
TO COME INTO YOUR OWN

BUT WHEN YOU'RE DYING IN AMERICA
AT THE END OF THE MILLENNIUM
YOU'RE NOT ALONE

I'M NOT ALONE
I'M NOT ALONE

(Blackout. Once again the phone rings.)

39. Voice Mail #5

ROGER and MARK'S ANSWERING MACHINE
SPEAK
(BEEEP!)

ROGER'S MOTHER
ROGER
THIS IS YOUR MOTHER
ROGER, HONEY, I DON'T GET THESE POSTCARDS
"MOVING TO SANTA FE"
"BACK IN NEW YORK"
"STARTING A ROCK BAND"
ROGER, WHERE ARE YOU??
PLEASE CALL

(The following is sung simultaneously.)

MIMI'S MOTHER
MIMI, CHICA, DONDÉ ESTA?
TU MAMA ESTA ILAMANDO
DONDÉ ESTAS, MIMI, CALL?

MR. JEFFERSON
KITTEN—WHEREVER ARE YOU—CALL

MRS. COHEN
MARK—ARE YOU THERE—ARE YOU THERE
I DON'T KNOW IF HE'S THERE

WE'RE ALL HERE WISHING YOU WERE HERE, TOO
WHERE ARE YOU, MARK, ARE YOU THERE, ARE YOU, WHERE ARE
YOU? MARK—ARE YOU THERE—ARE YOU THERE
I DON'T KNOW IF—PLEASE CALL YOUR MOTHER

40. Finale A

The lot and the loft

ALL SEVEN HOMELESS PEOPLE
CHRISTMAS BELLS ARE RINGING
CHRISTMAS BELLS ARE RINGING
CHRISTMAS BELLS ARE RINGING

HOW TIME FLIES
WHEN COMPASSION DIES

NO STOCKINGS
NO CANDY CANES
NO GINGERBREAD
NO SAFETY NET
NO LOOSE CHANGE
NO CHANGE NO

ONE HOMELESS MAN
SANTY CLAUS IS COMING

ALL
'CAUSE SANTY CLAUS AIN'T COMING

NO ROOM AT THE HOLIDAY INN—AGAIN
WELL, MAYBE NEXT YEAR
OR—WHEN

(Lights shift back to the loft. A small projector sits on a milk crate,
which sits on a dolly.)

MARK
DECEMBER 24, TEN PM EASTERN STANDARD TIME
I CAN'T BELIEVE A YEAR WENT BY SO FAST
TIME TO SEE—WHAT WE HAVE—TIME TO SEE
TURN THE PROJECTOR ON

(A rough title credit, "TODAY 4 U: Proof Positive" Appears, followed by a shot of ROGER tuning his guitar last Christmas.)

FIRST SHOT ROGER
WITH THE FENDER GUITAR HE JUST GOT OUT OF HOCK
WHEN HE SOLD THE CAR
THAT TOOK HIM AWAY AND BACK

ROGER
I FOUND MY SONG

MARK
HE FOUND HIS SONG
IF HE COULD JUST FIND MIMI

ROGER
I TRIED—YOU KNOW I TRIED

(MARK'S image appears on the screen.)

MARK
FADE IN ON MARK
WHO'S STILL IN THE DARK

ROGER
BUT HE'S GOT GREAT FOOTAGE

MARK
WHICH HE'S CUT TOGETHER

ROGER
TO SCREEN TONIGHT

(BENNY'S image appears on the screen.)

                    MARK
IN HONOR OF BENNY'S WIFE

                    ROGER
MUFFY
                    MARK
ALISON
PULLING BENNY OUT OF THE EAST VILLAGE LOCATION

(The projector blows a fuse. Blackout.)

                    ROGER
Then again. Maybe we won't screen it tonight.

                    MARK
I wonder how Alison found out about Mimi?

                    ROGER
Maybe a little bird told her.

(COLLINS enters in the dark, with twenty-dollar bills in each hand.)

                    COLLINS
Or an angel.

(Lights fade up.)

I HAD A LITTLE HUNCH THAT YOU COULD USE A LITTLE `FLOW

                    ROGER
TUTORING AGAIN?

                    COLLINS
NEGATIVE

                    MARK
BACK AT NYU?

COLLINS
NO, NO, NO
I REWIRED THE ATM AT THE FOOD EMPORIUM
TO PROVIDE AN HONORARIUM TO ANYONE WITH THE CODE

ROGER and MARK
THE CODE—
WELL . . . ?

COLLINS
A-N-G-E-L

YET ROBIN HOODING ISN'T THE SOLUTION
THE POWERS THAT BE MUST BE UNDERMINED WHERE THEY
DWELL
IN A SMALL, EXCLUSIVE GOURMET INSTITUTION
WHERE WE OVERCHARGE THE WEALTHY CLIENTELE

ALL THREE
LET'S OPEN A RESTAURANT IN SANTA FE
WITH A PRIVATE CORNER BANQUETTE, IN THE BACK
WE'LL MAKE IT YET, WE'LL SOMEHOW GET TO SANTA FE

ROGER
BUT YOU'D MISS NEW YORK BEFORE YOU COULD UNPACK

ALL
OHH—

(MAUREEN and JOANNE enter, carrying MIMI.)

MAUREEN
MARK! ROGER! ANYONE—HELP!

MARK
MAUREEN?

MAUREEN
IT'S MIMI—I CAN'T GET HER UP THE STAIRS

ROGER

NO!

(They enter the loft.)

MAUREEN

SHE WAS HUDDLED IN THE PARK IN THE DARK
AND SHE WAS FREEZING
AND BEGGED TO COME HERE

ROGER

OVER HERE
OH, GOD

(They lay her down carefully on the table.)

MIMI

GOT A LIGHT—I KNOW YOU—YOU'RE SHIVERING . . .

JOANNE

SHE'S BEEN LIVING ON THE STREET

ROGER

WE NEED SOME HEAT

MIMI

I'M SHIVERING

MARK

WE CAN BUY SOME WOOD AND SOMETHING TO EAT

COLLINS

I'M AFRAID SHE NEEDS MORE THAN HEAT

MIMI

I HEARD THAT

MAUREEN

COLLINS WILL CALL FOR A DOCTOR, HONEY

MIMI

DON'T WASTE YOUR MONEY ON MIMI, ME, ME

COLLINS

HELLO—911?
I'M ON HOLD

MIMI

COLD . . . COLD . . . WOULD YOU LIGHT MY CANDLE?

ROGER

YES, WE'LL, OH GOD—FIND A CANDLE

MIMI

I SHOULD TELL YOU
I SHOULD TELL YOU

ROGER

I SHOULD TELL YOU
I SHOULD TELL YOU

MIMI

I SHOULD TELL YOU
BENNY WASN'T ANY—

ROGER

SHHH—I KNOW

I SHOULD TELL YOU WHY I LEFT
IT WASN'T CAUSE I DIDN'T—

MIMI

I KNOW
I SHOULD TELL YOU

ROGER

I SHOULD TELL YOU

MIMI
(whispering)

I SHOULD TELL YOU
I LOVE YOU—

(MIMI fades.)

ROGER

WHO DO YOU THINK YOU ARE?
LEAVING ME ALONE WITH MY GUITAR
HOLD ON—THERE'S SOMETHING YOU SHOULD HEAR
IT ISN'T MUCH BUT IT TOOK ALL YEAR

(MIMI stirs and ROGER begins playing acoustic guitar at her bedside.)

41. Your Eyes

ROGER

YOUR EYES
AS WE SAID OUR GOODBYES
CAN'T GET THEM OUT OF MY MIND
AND I FIND I CAN'T HIDE (FROM)

YOUR EYES
THE ONES THAT TOOK ME BY SURPRISE
THE NIGHT YOU CAME INTO MY LIFE
WHERE THERE'S MOONLIGHT
I SEE YOUR EYES

(The band takes over.)

HOW'D I LET YOU SLIP AWAY
WHEN I'M LONGING SO TO HOLD YOU
NOW I'D DIE FOR ONE MORE DAY
'CAUSE THERE'S SOMETHING I SHOULD HAVE TOLD YOU
YES, THERE'S SOMETHING I SHOULD HAVE TOLD YOU

WHEN I LOOKED INTO YOU EYES
WHY DOES DISTANCE MAKE US WISE?
YOU WERE THE SONG ALL ALONG
AND BEFORE THE SONG DIES

I SHOULD TELL YOU I SHOULD TELL YOU
I HAVE ALWAYS LOVED YOU
YOU CAN SEE IT IN MY EYES

(We hear Musetta's theme, correctly and passionately. MIMI's head
falls to the side and her arm drops limply off the edge of the table.)

MIMI!

42. Finale B

(Suddenly MIMI's hand regains movement. Incredibly she's still alive.)

MIMI
I jumped over the moon!!

ROGER
What?

MIMI
A leap of Moooooooooooo—

JOANNE
She's back!

MIMI
I was in a tunnel. Heading for this warm, white light . . .

MAUREEN
Oh my God!

MIMI

And I swear Angel was there—and she looked good. And she said, "Turn around, girlfriend—and listen to that boy's song . . ."

COLLINS

SHE'S DRENCHED

MAUREEN

HER FEVER'S BREAKING

MARK

THERE IS NO FUTURE—THERE IS NO PAST

ROGER

THANK GOD THIS MOMENT'S NOT THE LAST

MIMI and ROGER

THERE'S ONLY US
THERE'S ONLY THIS
FORGET REGRET OR LIFE IS YOURS TO MISS

ALL

NO OTHER ROAD NO OTHER WAY
NO DAY BUT TODAY

(As the finale grows, the entire COMPANY makes its way onstage.)

WOMEN	MEN
I CAN'T CONTROL	WILL I LOSE MY DIGNITY
MY DESTINY	WILL SOMEONE CARE
I TRUST MY SOUL	WILL I WAKE TOMORROW
MY ONLY GOAL	FROM THIS NIGHTMARE
IS JUST TO BE	

(Mark's film resumes, along with two more films projecting on the back wall, "Scenes from *Rent* . . .")

WOMEN	MEN
WITHOUT YOU	THERE'S ONLY NOW
THE HAND GROPES	THERE'S ONLY HERE
THE EAR HEARS	GIVE IN TO LOVE
THE PULSE BEATS	OR LIVE IN FEAR
LIFE GOES ON	NO OTHER PATH
BUT I'M GONE	NO OTHER WAY
'CAUSE I DIE WITHOUT YOU	
I DIE WITHOUT YOU	NO DAY BUT TODAY
I DIE WITHOUT YOU	NO DAY BUT TODAY
I DIE WITHOUT YOU	NO DAY BUT TODAY
I DIE WITHOUT YOU	NO DAY BUT TODAY
I DIE WITHOUT YOU	NO DAY BUT TODAY
NO DAY BUT TODAY	

Biographies

JONATHAN LARSON (book, music, and lyrics) received the 1996 Pulitzer Prize for Drama for *Rent*. He also won the 1996 Tony Award for Best Musical and the 1994 Richard Rodgers Award for *Rent* and twice received The Gilman and Gonzalez-Falla Theatre Foundation's Commendation Award. In 1988, he won the Richard Rodgers Development Grant for his rock musical *Superbia*, which was staged at Playwrights Horizon. In 1989, he was granted the Stephen Sondheim Award from the American Music Theatre Festival, where he contributed to the musical *Sitting on the Edge of the Future*. He composed the score for the musical *J.P. Morgan Saves the Nation*, which was presented by En Garde Arts in 1995. Mr. Larson performed his rock monologue *tick, tick . . . BOOM!* at Second Stage Theatre, the Village Gate, and New York Theatre Workshop. In addition to scoring and songwriting for *Sesame Street*, he created music for a number of children's book-cassettes, including Steven Spielberg's *An American Tail* and *The Land Before Time*. Other film scores include work for *Rolling Stone* magazine publisher Jann Wenner. He conceived, directed, and wrote four original songs for *Away We Go!*, a musical video for children. *Rent,* his rock opera based on *La Bohème,* had its world premiere on February 13, 1996, at New York Theatre Workshop. Mr. Larson died unexpectedly of an aortic aneurysm on January 25, 1996, ten days before his thirty-sixth birthday.

VICTORIA LEACOCK HOFFMAN (Introduction) is a producer, filmmaker, and writer. She collaborated with Jonathan Larson, the creator of *Rent,* for over a decade. In 2001, she produced Larson's award-winning musical *tick, tick . . . BOOM!* Off-Broadway. She directed the music video "Kiki and Herb: Total Eclipse of the Heart" and is executive producer of the CD *Kiki and Herb Will Die for You at Carnegie Hall*. Her book *Signature Flowers: A Revealing Collection of Celebrity Drawings* was released in 1998. She co-founded Love Heals, the Alison Gertz Foundation for AIDS Education and is a founding board member of the Jonathan Larson Performing Arts Foundation. She is currently producing the feature film *I Heard That* by her husband Cal Hoffman.